THE MINISTRY AND MISSION OF
SUNG PRAYER

DAVID HAAS

ST. ANTHONY MESSENGER PRESS

Cincinnati, Ohio

Nihil Obstat: Rev. Thomas Richstatter, O.F.M.
         Rev. David L. Zink

Imprimi Potest: Rev. Fred Link, O.F.M.
         Provincial

Imprimatur: +Most Rev. Carl K. Moeddel, V.G.
         Archdiocese of Cincinnati
         December 10, 2001

The *nihil obstat* and *imprimatur* are a declaration that a book is considered to be free from doctrinal or moral error. It is not implied that those who have granted the *nihil obstat* and *imprimatur* agree with the contents, opinions or statements expressed.

Scripture quotations, unless otherwise noted, are from the *New Revised Standard Version Bible*, copyright ©1989 by the Division of Christian Education of the National Council of the Churches of Christ in the U.S.A. Used with permission. All rights reserved.

The chart on pages 61-62, copyright ©2001, The Emmaus Center for Music, Prayer and Ministry, 1595 Blackhawk Lake Drive, Eagan, MN 55122, is used with permission. All rights reserved.

We are grateful for permission to quote material printed by the following publishers: Reprinted by permission of OCP Publications, excerpts from Bernadette Farrell's "God Has Chosen Me" and "God Beyond All Names," copyright ©1990, Tom Conry's "I Will Not Die," copyright ©1984, 1990, Rory Cooney's "Bread of Life," copyright ©1987, "Song of the Chosen," copyright ©1984 and "Servant Song," copyright ©1987, Huub Oosterhuis' "Song to Jesus Christ," copyright ©1972, 1984, and "You," copyright ©1973, Bob Hurd's "In the Breaking of Bread," copyright ©1984 and Michael Joncas' "On Eagle's Wings," copyright ©1979. Reprinted by permission Hope Publishing Company, Brian Wren's "Dear Mother God," copyright ©1980 and "How Shall I Sing to God?," copyright ©1986 and Shirley Erena Murray's "Star-Child," copyright ©1994. Reprinted by permission of GIA Publications, Inc., excerpts from David Haas' "I Want to Call You," copyright ©1989, "Deep Down I Know," copyright ©1993, "God of All Creation," copyright ©1988, "What Is Your Name," copyright ©1991, "We Have Seen and We Have Heard," copyright ©1991, "Song of the Body of Christ," copyright ©1989, "You Are Mine," copyright ©1991, "We Are Called," copyright ©1988, Rory Cooney's "Magnificat," copyright ©1991, and "Walk in the Reign," copyright ©1990, Jeremy Young's "We Shall Rise Again," copyright ©1987, and Marty Haugen's "Spirit Blowing Through Creation," copyright ©1987 and "God of Day and God of Darkness, copyright ©1985, ©1994. Reprinted by permission of Pastoral Press, excerpts from Gerard Pottenbaum's *The Rites of People: Exploring the Ritual Character of Human Experience*, copyright ©1992 and *The Milwaukee Symposia for Church Composers: A Ten Year Report* copyright ©1992. Reprinted by permission of the United States Catholic Conference, Inc., excerpts from *Music in Catholic Worship*, copyright ©1983, *Environment and Art in Catholic Worship*, copyright ©1978 and *Liturgical Mass Today,* copyright ©1982.

Library of Congress Cataloging-in-Publication Data

Haas, David.
  The ministry and mission of sung prayer / David Haas.
    p. cm.
  ISBN 0-86716-214-7 (pbk.)
  1. Church music—Catholic Church. 2. Ministers of music. I. Title.
  ML3002 .H26 2002
  264'.0202—dc21

               2001006000

Cover and book design by Constance Wolfer
ISBN 0-86716-214-7

CONTENTS

PRELUDE

THIS IS A BOOK OF CONVICTIONS. These convictions are grounded in years of parish experience as a parish music and liturgy director, and as an observer, workshop leader, student of the liturgy and consultant. At the heart of my convictions is the notion that the ministry of music is more than the acquiring of specific skills and competencies in music and liturgical celebration. The ministry of music must be seen as a true vocation, one that leads and agitates both the minister and the people served to be sent forth in mission. Over the years I have come to the awareness that for many people, the term "ministry" is not necessarily synonymous with mission and discipleship. I believe ministry with the absence of a sense of mission is heretical and dangerous. It is this conviction that influenced the title of this book.

The stakes are high in this regard for those of us entrusted with the ministry of music. Since the Second Vatican Council, Roman Catholicism has seen great growth and promise in the renewal of the liturgy. In recent years, however, I have sensed a more pragmatic approach to the calling of music ministry in parishes, and this is due to many factors. An authentic sense of ministry has often been overshadowed by the need of full-time music ministers to be "professional" or "career"-centered in their activities. Job descriptions, salary negotiations, professional development, health benefits, days off and self-care, while vitally important and just issues for full-time ministers, have often consumed the concerns of those who are charged with leading people in sung prayer. Part-time or volunteer musicians also are pulled in so many different directions, that they and all of us are often unable to embrace the deeper calling that is grounded in our baptism and illuminated through our musical gifts and craft. Many music ministers are exhausted, burned-out and cynical. In recent years, the church has experienced an exodus of people from pastoral life to other pursuits.

We music ministers (like all people in ministry) are busy people, with too much to do, too much to think about and too much to juggle in the parallel lives of parish, home, family and musical interests. Much is asked of us, by our pastors, by our choir members and fellow music ministers, and by the parish at large. Some of us lead music at four or more liturgies a weekend; manage, plan and direct two to three rehearsals during the week; attend more meetings than we care to admit to; and meet with at least one or two engaged couples during the week to plan their wedding. The Rite of Christian Initiation of Adults (RCIA) director, or the director of formation, of course, wants us to lead a song for a formation evening, or offer training or in-service for catechists, and the youth minister has a youth Mass coming up and needs our help. And if that were not enough, there are two funerals that just got scheduled in an already over-scheduled, overwhelming week.

Sometimes people look at us and wonder why we do what we do. We seem to have no life—

we work on weekends, have daytime and evening events and schedules. We rarely get to worship purely as a member of the assembly—we almost never get to sit with our own family at church. Some people in the parish complain about what we are doing; we are constantly trying to build up, affirm and resolve conflicts among the people in our choirs and ensembles. The turfs between the "traditional" and "contemporary" choirs have become more entrenched, and the pastor, in some cases, seems to circumvent and unilaterally change and reverse some of the goals that we music ministers have sweated and bled for. We sometimes wonder ourselves, why do we endure the abuse?

We do so, hopefully, for one reason and one reason only: Jesus Christ. The "word made flesh" has penetrated our lives, blessed us all with the gift of music and stirred in us the desire and call to offer it back to the people of God. The hard work and sweat that we endure is at the center of ministry. Chapter 15 of the Gospel of John lays it out for us: "to lay down one's life for one's friends." Many music ministers who have professional competence may lose or forget to consider this deeper dimension.

Ministers are people who bend to wash the feet of their friends. Ministers are missionaries and, ironically, powerless people who face their own weakness without fear and make it available to others. It is this creative weakness that gives ministry energy and momentum. As music ministers, we have the unique vehicle of music to communicate, proclaim, provoke and nurture this notion and, as we know, the cost to do so is high. But we are called to do so, just the same. Why do we lay down our lives? There is one answer only: to give new life. To be a music minister is to be more than a professionally skilled person. It cannot be a job. It is a way of life, and a way of life for others to see, understand and to join with. To sing on this journey is to help to bring about the freedom and liberation that our baptism compels us to join in shaping and celebrating.

Throughout this book, I use Scripture as an important source of reflection and challenge. I believe that, in addition to our musical and liturgical skill-building, we need to delve more deeply into biblical wisdom for our ministerial journey. The Word frees us to abandon our sense of unworthiness enough to even consider that we might be ministers. We feel that we are not up to the task—we would much rather just be musicians. We feel that trying to develop a sense of worthiness is a useless enterprise, and that we will never achieve such a sense. But our baptism and our vocation provoke us to be ministers, and in reading the Scriptures we receive a glimpse into God's plan and strategy: God does not choose perfect people. If perfection were the prerequisite, there would be no ministers at all. The God of our Judaic and Christian faith did not use the criterion of unparalleled excellence. Let's take a look at some of the "worthy" people, whom God called forth:

MOSES. This man was "slow of tongue," in other words, needing help from Aaron and others. Yet he led his people to the Promised Land.

JEREMIAH. Too young.

DAVID. Too short.

JOB. Manic-depressive.

JONAH. Reluctant.

ZACCHEUS. Hated and reviled.

MARY MAGDALENE. Scorned.

PETER. This man is the ultimate "screw-up" of the Gospels. He wants to build tents at Mount Tabor (as we often like to do at liturgy) rather than live the daily life of discipleship. He panics on the lake when the storm gets out of hand. He gets squeamish when Jesus wants to wash his feet. He has heroic visions of Arnold Schwarzenegger- and Luke Skywalker-type behavior when the soldiers come to arrest Jesus. And he denies even knowing who Jesus is. This is the man we believe was our first pope. We refer to him as "rock of the church." How about a "quivering bowl of Jell-O" until the Holy Spirit got hold of him?

Who does God call? All of us: the screw-ups, the sinners, the weak and the vulnerable. We are called to give tirelessly (even when we are exhausted) of ourselves, our talents, our skills and our convictions in order to help people pray and celebrate authentically for the sake of mission for the life of the world. Sound a bit lofty? You bet. Our work and our charge is a lofty task, indeed.

When we look to the New Testament for a vision of ministry, Mary and John the Baptist are role models for the mission laid out before us. They are mentors especially for those of us in the ministry of music because their life response is celebrated in two of the most beloved biblical canticles, the Magnificat and the Benedictus.

Mary is a teenage girl (an unlikely vessel) chosen to be the primary agent for God breaking into our world. But she does so more than just biologically. One of Mary's titles is Theotokos, which means "God-bearer." She sends us on mission by her yes to the mission to which she was commissioned, and gives us a primal liturgical composition as the foundational music for our call:

My soul magnifies the Lord,
    and my spirit rejoices in God my savior,
for he has looked with favor on the lowliness of his servant.
    Surely, from now on all generations will call me blessed;
for the Mighty One has done great things for me,
    and holy is his name.
His mercy is for those who fear him
    from generation to generation.
He has shown strength with his arm;
    he has scattered the proud in the thoughts of their hearts.
He has brought down the powerful from their thrones,
    and lifted up the lowly;
he has filled the hungry with good things,
    and sent the rich away empty.
He has helped his servant Israel,
    in remembrance of his mercy,
according to the promise he made to our ancestors,
    to Abraham and to his descendants forever. *(Luke 1:46–55)*

Like John the Baptist, music ministers are people who continually point beyond themselves to Jesus Christ, and are thought of as being strange for doing so. We are called to prepare the way of the Lord, clearly acknowledging that Jesus is Lord and we are not. We should sing and dance, and act outrageously, like John, in the good news and relief that comes with knowing that we are not the savior. Rather, our responsibility is to "point," like he did, to Jesus. The true minister of music is one who helps us to remember the message of our song, rather than the messenger, him or herself. Zechariah foresaw the mission of John the Baptist to point beyond himself. The same is true for us:

> Blessed be the Lord God of Israel,
> > for he has looked favorably on his people and redeemed them.
> He has raised up a mighty savior for us
> > in the house of his servant David,
> as he spoke through the mouth of his holy prophets from of old,
> > that we would be saved from our enemies and from the hand of all who hate us.
> Thus he has shown the mercy promised to our ancestors,
> > and has remembered his holy covenant,
> the oath that he swore to our ancestor Abraham,
> > to grant us that we, being rescued from the hands of our enemies,
> might serve him without fear, in holiness and righteousness
> > before him all our days.
> And you, child, will be called the prophet of the Most High;
> > for you will go before the Lord to prepare his ways,
> to give knowledge of salvation to his people
> > by the forgiveness of their sins.
> By the tender mercy of our God,
> > the dawn from on high will break upon us,
> to give light to those who sit in darkness and in the shadow of death,
> > to guide our feet into the way of peace. *(Luke 1:68–79)*

Music ministry as a way of life, and not just musical and liturgical competence, can only happen when we are willing to deny ourselves in order to create the space where God can work. The challenge of the ministry and mission of music is to help offer a voice in which the spiritual desire of worshippers can make sense to them; in which the seeds of healing, liberation and the challenge to serve can be planted. This requires more than skills. This demands surrender and obedience.

Music ministry should never be seen as a service profession. Music ministry is a musical, affective and grateful response of God's people. It is not something we "do" or "provide" for someone else. It is a holy way of living and expression of our way of living for God and one another.

My hope is that *The Ministry and Mission of Sung Prayer* is more than a teaching tool or resource. My hope is that it can also be a prayerful journal, a touchstone for reflection that you as a music minister can come back to time and time again. While the chapters here contain specific liturgical background in documentation and principles and sections on specific musical considerations for implementation of music in worship, I have included source material, scriptural reflections and other insights to help us grow as missionaries for the beliefs of which we sing. I mince no words in these pages. My convictions are strong, and I state them passionately because I believe in them with all my heart.

Many people have influenced my thinking on these topics, and I am grateful to them. The thoughts and principles outlined in this book are a result of years of ministry in various settings, and anything I have offered here has been deeply influenced by people who have befriended me, taught and formed me, and endured me. While there are too many people to mention, I want to give thanks especially to the memory, light and life of Madelin Sue Martin, who planted within me and many others a holistic vision of music ministry and the formational issues for those entrusted with this calling. I am thankful to God for the living spirits of such wonderful liturgical and musical saints as Leon Roberts, Ralph Kiefer, Gene Walsh, Mike Hay and James Dunning, who taught me more about liturgy, music and faith than I can express. Special thanks to James Bessert and Michael Joncas, two of my first teachers in liturgy, for their knowledge, witness and love of ritual prayer. I thank the following friends and colleagues in music ministry and liturgy from whom I have learned much and who continue to inspire me through their toil, conviction and example: Mary Werner, Bob Batastini, Jim Moudry, Marty Haugen, Tom Franzak, Kate Cuddy, Ray East, Bob Hurd, Tony Alonso, Rob Glover, Stephen Petrunak, Joe Camacho, Derek Campbell, Carol Porter, Frank Brownstead, Dan Schutte, Virgil Funk, Barb Conley-Waldmiller, Mike Cymbala, Fred Moleck, Steve Pischner, Bobby Fisher, Kathy Jellison, Leisa Anslinger, Ed Foley, Donna Pena, Jo Infante, Dan Westmoreland, Michael Glaeser, Donna Hanna, Don Neumann, Christopher Walker, Nancy Bannister, Rory Cooney, Jeffrey Judge, John Foley, Denise Williby, Alissa Hetzner, Bonnie Faber, Tish Blain, Rembert Weakland, Paul Covino, Andrea Goodrich, Jo Mabini Greene, Thom Morris, Joe Wise, Betsey Beckman, Jackie Witter, Jim Waldo, Paulette Ching, Rob Strusinski, Fran O'Brien, Eileen Bird, Bob Duggan, Ricky Manalo, Ken Untener, Ray Kemp, Paul Jaroszeski, Jeanne Dold, Jim McCormick, Gary Daigle, Tom Kendzia, Mary Janus, Robin Medrud-Thul and Vicky Tufano. Deep thanks go to Lori True for ideas, input and insight, and to Arthur Zannoni, who has helped me realize and experience the importance of Scripture in formation, regardless of the ministerial discipline. Thanks to Helen Haas and Tom Richstatter, O.F.M., for reading the manuscript for this book and offering helpful comments. Thanks also to Dan Kantor, Marianne Bryan, Andrea Lee and Alec Harris for their support and encouragement. I want to thank Roberta Kolasa, Bill Huebsch, Gertrude Foley, Kate Kuenstler, George DeCosta, Anita Bradshaw, Helen Prejean and Kathleen Storms, who have truly challenged me to explore the deeper and ethical dimensions of my ministerial responsibility. And, of course, love and thanks to my parents, who loved me into being, for their lives of joy and song and for instilling music in my heart.

Like many liturgical compositions that I have attempted to create, this book was not easy to write. Most of my teaching in the areas of liturgy and music has been in workshops and seminars, and has evolved, changed (for the better, I hope!) and grown. I am a musician and a pastoral practitioner, not a theologian. I am also more of a talker than a writer, so creating a manuscript that would not sound like an extrovert rambling on paper was an even more daunting task. My deepest thanks must be expressed to the people of St. Anthony Messenger Press, especially my editor, April Bolton, and dear friend, Lisa Biedenbach. Their support, generosity and belief in my work (and inspirational patience in waiting for me to complete this manuscript) is humbling and a true gift. Their commitment to serving the people of God is truly inspiring to me, and I am proud to be a part of their mission.

Finally, I want to thank all of you who are engaged in the ministry of music, regardless of whether you serve as full-time director, or as volunteer member of the choir or ensemble. What you do is so important, and I thank God for your gifts, your sacrifice and your commitment to your vocation. It is to each of you that I dedicate this book. I hope and pray that *The Ministry and Mission of Sung Prayer* enriches your efforts and plays a small part in helping you to proclaim more passionately the great song of our faith: Jesus Christ, who lives and reigns forever and ever.

David Haas
The Emmaus Center for Music, Prayer and Ministry
Eagan, Minnesota
February 3, 2001, Feast of Saint Blaise

CHAPTER ONE

REFLECTIONS ON LITURGY AND RITUAL

It is madness to wear ladies' straw hats and velvet hats to church; we should all be wearing crash helmets. Ushers should issue life preservers and signal flares; they should lash us to our pews. For the sleeping God may wake someday and take offense, or the waking God may draw us out to where we can never return. —*Annie Dillard*[1]

WHY DO WE NEED LITURGY? What is liturgy? I believe that most of us rarely ask these kinds of questions. In my own story, liturgy was a centerpiece of my life before I even knew that such a question existed. These kinds of lofty questions were never part of my consciousness. I did not ask what "liturgy" was, I just went to church and participated in it regularly from childhood on. I enjoyed it. In fact, I loved it. My earliest memories growing up were centered in the church and its worship.

I grew up in a musical family. Both of my parents were parish musicians, and as long as I can remember, I was sitting next to my dad on the organ bench, playing a make-believe organ on the kneeler top next to the organ console. My parents were the typical volunteer parish musicians who sometimes did three to four liturgies on a Sunday with no pay, but totally in love with their involvement. As early as age six or seven, I would step up to the microphone with my boy soprano voice and sing the "Ave Maria" as a prelude to the Mass. As I grew older, I also became an altar boy, and after assisting in serving Communion, I would walk over to the organ and sing a solo. When I was in junior high, my brother and I were servers at one liturgy, helping Mom and Dad at another Mass, and playing guitar and singing with the newly formed "folk" group at another. Sunday was "church" day, and as a family we loved it, looked forward to it and were nurtured by it, even though we never were forced or asked to articulate or reflect upon how and why. I was formed into the faith as a result of my early involvement as a musician and as a server. For me, my family and my parish community, the liturgy was an anchor.

Most of us who are involved as music ministers have similar stories of how we were formed into this ministry—not through learning or studying—but rather, by being involved, by being mentored into this activity by parents or other adults. We went to church, and we were seduced by its wonder and the effects of belonging, and by participation. However, if we reflect more deeply upon the human experience of most members of our faith communities (and our own experience as liturgical leaders), we can learn much about what liturgy is and what people long for in their participation and involvement in liturgy.

WHAT DRAWS PEOPLE TO LITURGY

If we were to take a poll in an average parish and ask people their motivation in coming to Mass, we would end up with a variety of motivations and intentions. Some would say that they come to Mass out of fear—that is, because of the burden of the obligation to attend Sunday Mass. Some would say they are there because Mom and Dad are "making me go." Some come to church because they like to be "alone with God." Others would say they come because they love the sense of community and being with other people. Some would say they are there because of the wonderful, charismatic priest; others because they love the music. Still others come because they want to express gratitude for the blessings they have in their life—and some, just the opposite: They come because they are hurting and are searching for answers. There are many more reasons why people come to Mass on Sunday. We should not judge any of these motivations, but be honestly aware that they exist.

In our weekly experience, we see that there are many different answers that would arise from the question, "Why do we need the liturgy?" Liturgy is a time for quiet prayer and devotion for some. For others it is adult education, a time to learn about our beliefs and doctrines. Because of the reality of the human condition, and the strong self-help movement in our present American culture, some come to worship for therapy and help in the struggle of their lives. Most people come to liturgy with the desire to be inspired and uplifted. But while these are good reasons to come to church, and while the liturgy can serve many of these needs, they still in and of themselves do not express what the liturgy is or why we have the need to gather in ritual prayer.

Many liturgical scholars can answer the question of why we need the liturgy far better than I. Even among these scholars and other professionals, there is a wide variety of insights about why we worship and what is the goal of liturgical celebration for Christians. However, as ministers of sung prayer we need to grapple with the essence of liturgy and ritual before we can effectively apply our unique gifts of music to that enterprise. In other words, before we exercise our ministry of music, we need to at least be able to discuss and reflect on some basic values and principles of liturgy and its importance to the life of the church. Without some basic foundational values of liturgy, parish worship often is reduced to being defined by personal taste. For effective music ministry to be implemented, the following liturgical principles need to be heeded.

FOUNDATIONAL PRINCIPLES OF LITURGY

LITURGY IS A CELEBRATION OF FAITH

I once presented a workshop in which I boldly stated this principle, and a woman stood up and said, "not in my parish!" This is a sad commentary, indeed. Liturgy does not exist in a vacuum, for we have to remember that Jesus did not come to give us liturgy. Rather, Jesus came that we might have life! I would like to examine this understanding of liturgy as a "faith-response" by delineating three movements in the journey of faith of the early church.

FIRST MOVEMENT—EXPERIENCE

The early church began with an intense, passionate *experience* of Jesus—his teaching, his values, every aspect of his life. The early church lived and celebrated this experience through those who walked with Jesus and the early disciples that followed during the early post-resurrection period. At the heart of this first movement is conversion—Jesus had radically challenged the way in which people lived, what they believed and what was of value to them. He turned their lives upside down, and they were never the same again.

While many of these people knew the human Jesus of Nazareth personally, what truly transformed their lives was their experience of the *risen* Lord. This common experience of the risen Christ was shared and lived through lifestyle, service and a common life of prayer and community. Jesus gave the world hope and meaning. This led to a way of life that was unheard of before that time, and led to a renunciation of previous structures, patterns and moral codes. Yes, Jesus died for our sins, but Jesus also died because he said dangerous things; he interacted with the wrong people, boldly challenged the forces of power and called for repentance. For the early community, to "take on the way of Jesus" meant embracing this same witness, this same boldness and the same prophetic lifestyle.

We also have to remember that the early Christians were an illegal band of people, thought to be a dangerous cult by those in power. The early Christian community was persecuted and even martyred for their faith. They met in homes, often in hiding and in secret. To follow Jesus was very dangerous and to do so had immense consequences. In addition, when Jesus proclaimed his "coming again in glory," many in the early church thought that this time was just around the corner. When they began to realize that this would not be the case, their increased need and desire to gather became more intense and focused. There was a need to "remember" and recall the true memory of Jesus, to do what he did—to tell the story, to share the meal, to proclaim the Good News in a specific, intentional way.

SECOND MOVEMENT—RITUAL

At the center of these needs was the need to *celebrate* this experience—to ritualize and pray together as a result of what had already happened to them. Their lives were changed, and they were compelled to celebrate. This is a very natural and human response to good things that have happened for us—when we have a powerful and positive experience, we need to and we must celebrate in some way. For the early church, ritual was at the center of claiming and nurturing Christian identity in a time and culture that was hostile to the Jesus movement. It was a powerful act of solidarity and unity, and it flowed from a common experience. The form and structure of these rituals varied in detail, but the common element was a fervent experience of faith, with the foundation of word and meal at the center of these gatherings. The origin of liturgy was not a geographic location, not a building (as is the case in many canonical parishes today), but the common experience and commitment to the gathered community, the "Body of Christ."

THIRD MOVEMENT—CATECHESIS

The third movement after the journey of experience and ritual is catechesis, or *mystagogia*, a Greek term meaning "to break open the experience." That is to say, we have had this powerful experience of Christ in our lives and now we gather to celebrate this powerful transformation. What does it all mean? What can we learn from this experience? What is the wisdom that helps our experience? What leads us to real and lasting change and action? This is what "theology" means: "faith seeking understanding." In other words, experience moving beyond initial conversion to a sustained, ongoing change of heart and spiritual growth and wisdom.

In examining these three movements, we can see the problems with parish liturgy in our communities. Far too often, the faith journey moves in the opposite direction, that is, from ritual to experience. We begin by having our children attend Catholic schools or religious education programs with a mandated attendance at Sunday Mass. In the midst of this, we hope and desire that someday our children will experience something of such great magnitude that it changes their lives. Most believers are born into a Christian household. We are expected to go to church and learn our catechism. We have no fear or persecution for our beliefs, because unlike for the early church, these beliefs are in the cultural mainstream. Due in part to our busy lives, liturgy often becomes the place where we expect people to be given "an experience," and where we "teach" people about our faith and beliefs. This was never the intention of liturgy in the early church. In the early church liturgy and worship were expression and ritual activity that presumed experience and led people to a deepening of that faith in real life.

These expressions are given full status in liturgy that is true and authentic. True worship and praise contains the dynamics of all that we experience in life: joy, praise, hope, lament, anger, rage, reconciliation, tears. There is no single theme of the liturgy, except for the ongoing celebration of the paschal mystery, the true dying and rising in Christ, not only at the moment of initial conversion but throughout the entirety of our lives. As we proclaim at the Easter Vigil: "This is our faith, this is the faith of the church. We are proud to profess it in Jesus Christ our Lord."

LITURGY IS AN ACTION OF THE CHURCH, CELEBRATED BY THE ASSEMBLY

Simply and directly put: Liturgy is an action that we share *through* Christ, *with* Christ and *in* Christ. The document *Music in Catholic Worship (MCW)*, published by the Bishops' Committee on the Liturgy in 1983, contains a most eloquent and bold summary of why we gather for worship:

> We are Christians because through the Christian community we have met Jesus Christ, heard his word in invitation, and responded to him in faith. We gather at Mass that we may hear and express our faith again in this assembly and, by expressing it, renew and deepen it.[2]

We come to liturgy because in some way, through our own unique individual and collective stories, we have experienced the living Christ in our lives. We have, in either large or small ways, experienced a conversion—not necessarily a single moment of dramatic *metanoia*, but often a gradual awareness of a power greater than ourselves, through the many "dyings" and "risings" that are part of the path of following Jesus. As the late writer and priest Father James Dunning used to like to say, we are not "born again," but rather, "born again, and again, and again."

True conversion cannot stay silent and hidden. By its very nature, authentic change demands of us a bold proclamation in every part and expression of our lives. True conversion is always in need of nurturance, support and rekindling. We cannot do that alone. We need other members of the Christian "tribe" to walk with us, challenge us, pray and celebrate with us, and witness to us the way of living in the Spirit. To celebrate the joys of life, and to survive and rise above the terror of life, we need to gather around the stories of our God and each other. We need to make good rituals and signs.

In the midst of all things God is worthy of our worship. We glorify God, but not as a God who is far away from us, but rather one who is close and ever present. A popular song in recent memory speaks about a God who watches us "from a distance." Such sentiments are just downright heresy. We experience God through the risen one, the Christ, who is present not just in tabernacles, bread and wine, and in the Word, but in the midst of real human beings, in those we gather with and even in those we have yet to encounter. As the disciples welcomed the stranger on the road to Emmaus, we welcome and recognize the presence of Jesus in the midst of each other. We deepen our solidarity with the Body of Christ, so we may be better equipped to live and celebrate in action what the liturgy so boldly proclaims to us: "Go in peace to love and serve the Lord."

Due to our human circumstances, we need an ongoing community, and we gather not once, as if we were attending a seminar that would give us all of the information in one session, rather, we gather Sunday after Sunday. It is in this ongoing and repetitive act that we hear the stories over and over with a new awareness. In liturgy, we enter into an alternative rhythm and vision from what we often experience. It is an experience and a place where we can be strengthened for the journey. Liturgy is a place where all are welcomed regardless of what we think of ourselves, what the world may think of us, a place where all are accepted and embraced in love. Liturgy is where we gather as a diverse people. We listen to and embrace the great stories of faith in the Scriptures. We share in a meal that proclaims a foretaste of the reign of God, and we are sent forth to keep trying to integrate this vision into our lives. We repeat this same ritual with the hope that we may be brought closer to living with more integrity the conversion we experience.

As believers, we have been changed. We have experienced and been witness to the reality of Jesus Christ most profoundly in the hopes, dreams, fears, and dyings and risings in our lives. Because of Christ, we cannot live our lives in the same way. This presence and awareness of Jesus has been made real to us through creation, through our relationships, in the joys and trials that we have come to know. This presence calls forth in us the joy, and the challenge, to serve with all the passion that we possibly can muster. This passion compels us to dedicate our lives as a celebration of the presence of Jesus in all whom we encounter. The journey is difficult, and we need the presence of other believers to walk with us and challenge us along the way. Liturgy provides a grounding in which we can pray, celebrate and become empowered to live the gospel the best we can.

Another way to look at this is to ask, "Who 'does' the liturgy?" Even though the Second Vatican Council published their documents in the 1960s, it is amazing to note how little of the theology reflected in those writings has actually been felt in our parish communities. We as a church often articulate the jargon and rhetoric of "participation" and liturgy being the "work of the people," but the overwhelming reality is that we still have many people who believe and experience the liturgy as being celebrated by the priest alone, while we as an assembly "attend." We still want to know which priest is going to "say the Mass" and to find out who will be "doing the music."

The great conspiracy that still lurks in many of our parishes is that the assembly are the recipients of what is given to them by the power brokers, being not only the priest, but even the other ministries of music, reading and so on. The greatest task of the liturgical renewal is yet to be realized, for the great sleeping giant, the parish assembly, has yet, in most settings, truly to see, experience and invest themselves as the primary "actors" of the liturgical event. This is where our greatest strategies and creativity need to be summoned, but it is also the source of most of the difficulties we have regarding participation. Liturgy is not quiet time alone with God, but rather, ritual prayer and participation in community, the Body of Christ.

While personal prayer and devotion is fundamental in the life of every Christian, liturgy is about something more expansive. Liturgy is not about me—it is about "we."

In the Old Testament, the ongoing proclamation is: "… you shall be my people, and I will be your God" (see Jeremiah 31:33). This is a difficult message in our life today, especially in Western, U.S. culture. We live in a culture in love with individualism. We are deeply concerned with "what *I* want" and "what *I* need." It is this demon that finds its way into our life of faith especially in liturgy, where everyone seems to be an expert. We have to correct this notion. Our faith is not "between God and me." This is heresy. Your faith *is* my business, and my faith *is* your business. We are called to nurture, challenge and build up each other, and this is where liturgy is truly countercultural. The very word *liturgy* in its Greek roots means "common work of the people." In terms of participation and music ministry, this means that the primary minister of music is not the cantor, choir or instrumentalist—but rather, the gathered assembly. This musically untrained congregation is the primary minister of sung prayer.

The assembly is not going to sing or participate and take ownership of the liturgy if they do not *experience **themselves** as the church.* Essential elements of quality liturgy include good music, good hymnals, quality sound systems, good acoustics, great choirs, and passionate readers and presiding priests and preachers. But no matter how good these things are, they will have only limited results if the people in the pews continue to see themselves as second-class citizens. The self-esteem of our people needs to be lifted so that they experience themselves as the presence of Christ. Music and the other elements of celebration will fail if there is not good hospitality, strong evangelization and catechesis pertaining to the role of the assembly.

This is not some radical new thought conjured by a bunch of crazy liturgists and troublemakers. This is the vision of *Lumen Gentium*, or *Dogmatic Constitution on the Church,* from the council fathers of Vatican II. Throughout the document, the church is passionately named the "people of God," a "sheepfold" and a "people brought into unity."

In the Scriptures we are given this same reverence: "For in the one Spirit we were all baptized into one body" (1 Corinthians 12:13); "Because there is one bread, we who are many are one body, for we all partake of the one bread" (1 Corinthians 10:17), and "individually we are members one of another" (Romans 12:5).

LITURGY UTILIZES A RICH DIVERSITY OF MINISTRIES

Within this tapestry of holy people, we have many diversified gifts among the members:

> Now there are varieties of gifts, but the same Spirit; and there are varieties of services, but the same Lord; and there are varieties of activities, but it is the same God who activates all of them in everyone. To each is given the manifestation of the Spirit for the common good. *(1 Corinthians 12:4–7)*

If liturgy is truly a communal experience, then the calling forth of these gifts through mentoring and ongoing formation is essential. Our former understanding and experience of the liturgy was that the priest did everything, and music was seen as window dressing at best.

The renewal of Vatican II has helped us to rediscover liturgy as an activity that must require and celebrate the community of servants, whose roles are in addition to the important role of the presiding priest. This community of servants includes ministers of the Word (lectors); hospitality ministers, of whom more is required than being simply ushers; ministers of the table, who bring the Eucharist to the gathering and to the sick and homebound; ministers of movement (that is, liturgical dance); music ministers (including cantors, choir members and instrumentalists); and those in other such important ministries as the environment, preparation and planning, music composing and serving. But in the midst of these various and important ministries, it is important always to point their energies and actions toward empowering the primary ministry of the gathered, praying assembly.

It is these many and glorious gifts that we bring to the liturgy. In fact, in some early cultures, community, or *communitas,* was understood to mean "the giving of gifts." We need to take a fresh look at our basic understanding of worship and roles; we need to make a severe paradigm shift. Although we sit in rows of pews in our worship spaces (I refuse to call the *building* a "church"), as if we were the audience, the opposite is true. To paraphrase Kierkegaard, "Worship is like drama, except that the congregation are the actors and players; the ministers are merely prompters, giving cues and suggestions from the wings; and the audience—is God."

LITURGY EMPLOYS A UNIQUE LANGUAGE OF RITUAL AND SYMBOL

Liturgy is a different form of gathering and communication. As *Music in Catholic Worship* states, "People in love make signs of love, not only to express their love but also to deepen it. Love never expressed dies. Christians' love for Christ and for one another and Christians' faith in Christ and in one another must be expressed in the signs and symbols of celebration or they will die" (*MCW* #4). The document continues, "...the signs and symbols of worship can give bodily expression to faith as we celebrate. Our own faith is stimulated. We become one with others whose faith is similarly expressed. We rise above our own feelings to respond to God in prayer" (*MCW* #5). In other words, symbolic and ritual language has the ability to rise above and permeate the shallowness, deceptions and limitations of mere spoken expression.

The word *ritual* can often evoke negative reactions from people. I believe this is so because we have been flooded so often with so many bad experiences of ritual, both in church environments and in other settings. Ritual, however, is necessary for our survival as human beings, and what we are often reacting to is badly done ritual. Ritual activity is part of the human fabric, common to all of us, often celebrating and intensifying the most elemental situations of human activity. The following story of a typical ritual event by a visitor to America I believe helps bring the point home.

You find yourself inside a home. The family is seated around a table. There are four children. It's hard to tell the difference between the boys and the girls; they dress in similar clothes and their hair is about the same length, though the boy's hair seems to be shorter. You wonder if the length of hair has anything to do with age and position, because the person seated at the end of the table has the shortest hair and he is the largest person there. He must be the father. The person in the next room with all of the storage cabinets on the walls must be the mother. She is preparing something with a fire on top.

She touches a button at the door and the lights go off. Then she enters, carrying the fire on a platter. You remember from previous reading about this culture that this must be what they call "cake." It is a sweet bread-like mixture with an even sweeter covering.

"Cake" is a special food that they eat at various celebrations. This one, you recall, is a birthday celebration; so they call this a "birthday cake." Every year, families celebrate each person's birthday. The candles of fire stand for the number of years the person has been alive. On the cake is usually written "Happy Birthday" and the person's name. The same sweet mixture is used to write these words as is used to cover the cake so that it all can be eaten.

The cake can be round or square, though some people prefer the round shape as it suggests unity and the oneness of life. The square cake is usually prepared when large numbers of people are present; it is flatter and easier to cut than is the taller, round cake.

On such occasions, it is important that everyone eat a piece of cake, even a small bite. This is so even for people who do not especially like the taste of cake, or who have joined certain organizations that follow strict dietary laws.

(These organizations are not to be confused with religious sects, though the people may pray when they meet. The organizations referred to here are concerned with people's health, such as one called "Weight Watchers" which helps people who have a weight problem. Unlike many other cultures, the weight problem here is one of having eaten too much, rather than too little.)

To refuse to eat of the cake is an insult to the person whose birthday is being celebrated. The cake is a sign of the person's life. To refuse the cake is to refuse the person. The birthday celebration is the way these people say without words to someone: "We're happy you were born. You bring brightness and warmth to us as to these candles. The longer you are with us, the brighter our lives glow with yours... as is marked by the growing number of candles year after year. We find you a pleasant person; you leave a good taste in our mouths as does this sweet food. We eat this food marked with your name to say we believe in you personally and in your goodness. We share this food to make tangible our belief that we are of one life, one body. We treasure and celebrate being united with you and with each other in human life."

The birthday celebration is also marked by a song which is sung as the cake is being brought in and before the candles are extinguished. On no other occasion is this song used.

> Happy birthday to you.
> Happy birthday to you.
> Happy birthday dear [person's name].
> Happy birthday to you.

After the song ends, the birthday person blows out the candles. But before that happens, the person makes a wish. It is said that if the person blows the candles out in one breath, the wish comes true. Although adults do not believe in any cause-and-effect relationship between blowing out the candles and whether or not the wish comes true, adults still perform the rite. In is an expression of hope in the life to come and, as some who have studied this culture believe, making a birthday wish can be interpreted as a sign of faith in a power greater than themselves.

The birthday person is further honored by being allowed to cut the first piece of cake. Even the very small child who cannot manage the knife will at least be allowed a hand on the knife's handle when the first cut is made. Or sometimes the small child is allowed to simply stick a finger into the carefully decorated cake. It is reported in some studies that should the child do this on any other special-cake occasion, the adult slaps the child's hand and sometimes sends the child to another room usually reserved for sleeping. This only highlights the seriousness with which these people take their special cakes and the keeping of certain rites surrounding the eating of these cakes.[3]

This delightful story outlines many elements that make up good ritual. Objects and elements are used for the celebration, including movement and procession, darkness and lighted candles, and words and songs that are deeply tied to the ritual experience. The event takes place not willy-nilly, but in a specific place at a specific time, and, very importantly, is performed by the people and from memory. Parts of the ritual express deep realities of the people who have gathered. The people who have come together to celebrate a birthday do not need a detailed commentary, like the one above, in order to understand what is being expressed—the ritual and the symbols, gestures and sounds of the experience do that well enough. The ritual expresses far better than a verbal description what needs to be communicated. This is ritual par excellence.

Ritual language can take the longings and truths of our lives and elevate them to a more profound level of understanding and clarity. The reason we spend so much time, energy and effort in the quest for quality liturgy is because we know and have experienced both the positive and the "dark" side of liturgical celebration. "Faith grows when it is well expressed in celebration. Good celebrations foster and nourish faith. Poor celebrations weaken and destroy it" (*MCW* #6).

The birthday story helps to reinforce important principles about ritual and symbol for Christian liturgical celebration:

RITUAL IS REPETITIVE AND FAMILIAR

Ritual is repetitive, done over and over again and at its best when done by heart. The experience is known and owned by the community. Certain repetitive gestures are "entry" gestures because of these qualities. An example in our Roman Catholic liturgy is the Sign of the Cross that begins the celebration. This ritual act is not mindless movement, but a signal and cue recognizable and owned by all. Out of good intentions to be creative, liturgists and others sometimes will replace the Sign of the Cross with some adaptation in language or gesture that leaves the assembly confused. That is the sort of reaction we may face when we attempt to tamper—at our own peril—with certain ritual gestures and texts. Such tampering can rob the assembly of their access to the event.

The repetitive nature of ritual often results in dismay among musicians and liturgists who believe strongly that "variety and change should rule the day." Frequent change of repertoire (especially of ritual music acclamations, for example) with the good intention of creating variety, results far too often in a parish assembly who cannot keep up. Too many parish assemblies become preoccupied with learning the new song, as opposed to being freed to enter into the ritual event on a deeper level. Liturgists and musicians need to be mindful of the tension between the value of fresh and new musical and ritual patterns, and the need for consistency and familiarity. The true nature of ritual is in the assembly coming to own the experience, not in their constantly wondering what will happen next.

SYMBOLS ARE ESSENTIAL TO RITUAL

Liturgy is expressed and celebrated in the language of the symbols at the heart of our tradition. At the heart of our Christian identity are what we often call "smells and bells." These actions are ineffective when they are celebrated carelessly. Try to imagine a liturgical celebration without bread and wine, water, oil, lighted candles, incense or the cross. Symbols hold our belief systems and in the Christian liturgy contain the basic lexicon for our common activity together.

SYMBOLS ARE PURPOSELY AMBIGUOUS, AND SHOULD NOT BE EXPLAINED

While liturgy should certainly be accessible, it should never seem or become fully understood or "knowable." The balance between transcendence/mystery and immanence/relevancy is often a centerpiece of debate. Both are needed, but far too often, well-intentioned liturgy planners want to make sure every one "understands" what is going on. We are especially concerned with this in regard to children and our youth. I remember a mother telling me once that she would never take her child to the Easter Vigil because her young one would not understand what was going on. I answered her by asking, "Do you understand what is going on?" Do any of us really know what is going on? Should we? The Vigil, our liturgical symbols (and our entire liturgical life for that matter) are not to be grasped in this way. When I was a young boy, my parents took me to the Easter Vigil, and while I did not truly understand what was going on, I was truly engaged in the experience. And as I grew older, my imagination and understanding grew and expanded, but to this day, I do not totally understand.

The lavish and wonderful symbolic resources of our liturgical life can never be reduced to one solitary meaning. Parents and teachers should resist the temptation to pass on to our children any definitive meaning of these actions. Who could honestly declare a single, clear definition of what the cross means, for example? Who could share in simple, direct language the true meaning of bread and wine in the sharing of the eucharistic feast?

The ritual and symbols of the liturgy are multivalent in meaning, and should be open-ended, not closed in intent and celebration. We should be less consumed with what the symbols mean, but instead, be concerned about how lavishly the symbols are being celebrated and proclaimed. When most people complain about ritual and symbol, they are concerned about rituals that possess no passion or flair, and are executed with no investment and energy. Our liturgical celebrations demand lavish and compelling symbols and ritual actions. When our ritual "performance" is done with this kind of care and attentiveness, then the awesome power and presence of our loving God can be seen and celebrated that much more authentically. When our liturgy is celebrated with these powerful actions, the assembly will be challenged to respond—challenged and provoked to a deeper level of thinking and action.

MUSIC IS SYMBOLIC AND RITUAL SPEECH

We need to claim the language of music as ritual speech. Unlike what we see in movie musicals, we do not normally sing to each other on the street. Part of the problem with the sung participation of the assembly is that music in our culture is more likely to be something we listen to rather than participate in, while in the liturgy, music becomes the language that we use to express our joy, praise and even our lamenting. Liturgy without music is not liturgy. Liturgical music that does not hold the assembly as its central voice is a contradiction in terms. Words that are sung are communicated more deeply than when they are merely recited. It is one thing to say, "I love you," but to sing these words is something else. It is one thing to say, "Alleluia!" but more complete and truthful when sung.

To sing is to use the language of the heart; to sing is to elevate our discourse:

Singing is discovered and invented, it is born at times when there is no other possible way for people to express themselves—at the grave, for example, when four or five people with untrained, clumsy voices sing words that are greater and smaller than their faith and their experience.[4]

Another important principle illustrated in the birthday story cited previously is that the music is known, owned and familiar to all who take part in the ritual. There is no need for explanation, everyone takes part and the community gathered is not self-conscious about their participation, unlike in many of our liturgical assemblies.

Second, the "ritual song" ("Happy Birthday to You") only makes sense in the context of the ritual itself. In other words, the song is so deeply tied to the ritual action that to utilize it in any other context would be ludicrous. In liturgy, we celebrate, acclaim and rejoice in our baptism. If this is true, how can we "keep from singing"? Singing is what is needed when we give praise, when we petition our God and when we process and share in the meal. We sing at ritual because we need to.

LITURGY EMPOWERS PEOPLE FOR MISSION AND DISCIPLESHIP

Liturgy does not exist for its own sake. We have to remember that we do not deepen and enrich our faith purely for our own selfish purposes. All worship and all ministry are bound up in the cause of mission. All of the activity and energy of the parish, whether it be for liturgy, religious education, the parish school, youth ministry or social ministry, is dedicated for the sake of the reign of God. Liturgy, in other words, should not give us a "massage" (or what Sister Joan Chittister has declared liturgy to be for some, a "spiritual Jacuzzi") that will make us just feel good, or feel good about each other.

Liturgy is not therapy, although certainly it has therapeutic results for many. Liturgy should propel us beyond ourselves. It should confront and challenge us with the task of *gospel living* for the sake of the reign of God. If this is not the ultimate goal of liturgy (and music ministry), then it should not exist. Every aspect of our liturgical ministry must keep this at the center and forefront of our efforts and goals. Otherwise, liturgy will be what it seems to be for many (resulting in many staying away), a pious and isolated event that really has no impact and makes no impression on the rest of the lives of the participants. The final words of every eucharistic celebration, "Go in peace to love and serve the Lord," is not just nice sentiment and a good way to bring an end to the celebration, but, rather, it is the very energy and activity that the *entire* liturgy calls all of us to embrace. These words should help us to reclaim our tradition, which has always held liturgy and social justice as true partners. Liturgy proclaims and celebrates faith, but also sends us forth to live that faith.

We do not celebrate the liturgy out of nostalgia or out of the need to preserve traditional forms for their own sake. The real tradition is Jesus Christ, who died, rose and is continually being revealed in our world and time. Liturgy should do more than just affirm certain values, or even encourage participation. We must through our ritual gatherings make a commitment to Jesus' values and do so in solidarity with one another.

I hate, I despise your festivals,
and I take no delight in your solemn assemblies.
Even though you offer me your burnt offerings and grain offerings,
I will not accept them;
and the offerings of well-being of your fatted animals
I will not look upon.
Take away from me the noise of your songs;
I will not listen to the melody of your harps.
But let justice roll down like waters,
    and righteousness like an ever-flowing stream. *(Amos 5:21-24)*

These words from the prophet Amos should make us quiver and shake. This prophetic challenge in many ways should be the true standard by which we evaluate our liturgical life: Do our celebrations truly provoke a change of life? Do they celebrate the status quo? Do they compel the community to be transformed and to act? When we have the courage to ask and respond to these questions and challenges then we will truly have a liturgy that is speaking, touching, singing and acting in God's name.

NOTES

[1] Annie Dillard, *Teaching a Stone to Talk: Expeditions and Encounters* (New York: Harper and Row, 1988), pp. 40-41.

[2] *Music in Catholic Worship,* Bishops' Committee on the Liturgy, United States Conference of Catholic Bishops, 1972, n. 1.

[3] Gerard Pottebaum, *The Rites of People: Exploring the Ritual Character of Human Experience,* rev. ed. (Portland, Ore.: The Pastoral Press, 1992), pp. 31-34.

[4] Huub Oosterhuis, *At Times I See: Reflections, Prayers, Poems and Songs* (New York: Herder and Herder, 1970), pp. 103-104.

CHAPTER TWO

*B*IBLICAL SOURCES FOR MUSIC MINISTRY

I will sing praises to my God all my life long. —*Psalm 146:2*

I BELIEVE WITH MY ENTIRE BEING that music always was, and still is, God's idea. That being the case, it is good to begin our ministerial reflection as music ministers by delving a bit into the Scriptures.

From the very beginning of creation, God created a covenant with humanity, and music was a primary language of that covenant, a connection that has kept God's relationship with the world vital, vibrant and passionate. At the primal moments of our biblical salvation history, music is always part of the story.

Our parents in faith foresaw the world and mystery that was to unfold, and saw the need for song to keep the journey alive. Those of us who are ministers of music have them to thank:

Adah bore Jabal; he was the ancestor of those who live in tents and have livestock. His brother's name was Jubal; he was the ancestor of all those who play the lyre and pipe. *(Genesis 4:20–21)*

When God helped our ancestors to live in hope and led them to new freedom, new life and new adventures, Moses, Miriam and the entire family of faith broke out the instruments and had a musical frenzy:

Then the prophet Miriam, Aaron's sister, took a tambourine in her hand; and all the women went out after her with tambourines and with dancing. And Miriam sang to them:
    Sing to the Lord, for he has triumphed gloriously;
    horse and rider he has thrown into the sea. *(Exodus 15:20–21)*

Musical liturgy did not begin with the renewal of the liturgy at the Second Vatican Council. Acclamations, musical shouts and litanies have always been the clarion call for those following in faith:

On the morning of the third day there was thunder and lightning, as well as a thick cloud on the mountain, and a blast of a trumpet so loud that all the people who were in the camp trembled. Moses brought the people out of the camp to meet God. They took their stand at the foot of the mountain. Now Mount Sinai was wrapped in smoke, because the Lord had descended upon it in fire; the smoke went up like the smoke of a kiln, while the whole mountain shook violently. As the blast of the trumpet grew louder and louder, Moses would speak and God would answer him in thunder. *(Exodus 19:16–19)*

When you go to war in your land against the adversary who oppresses you, you shall sound an alarm with the trumpets, so that you may be remembered before the LORD your God and be saved from your enemies. *(Numbers 10:9)*

The call to conversion has always been a powerful source for song; the call to repentance, forgiveness and embracing a new way of life has always required music:

…as you come to the town, you will meet a band of prophets coming down from the shrine with harp, tambourine, flute, and lyre playing in front of them; they will be in a prophetic frenzy. Then the spirit of the LORD will possess you, and you will be in a prophetic frenzy along with them and be turned into a different person. Now when these signs meet you, do whatever you see fit to do, for God is with you. *(1 Samuel 10:5–7)*

Music has always been a healing balm, par excellence. When we feel broken, spent, discouraged, depressed and hopeless, God gives us a song, a lyric, a melody that pulls us out of our darkness and propels us to new life, new possibilities, and renewal of mind, body and spirit. King David did more than compose many of the psalms—he mentored all of us in showing us a way to minister with our gift, and to offer that gift in response to God's generosity for the service of those who are in need of lifting up:

Now the spirit of the LORD departed from Saul, and an evil spirit from the LORD tormented him. And Saul's servants said to him, "See now, an evil spirit from God is tormenting you. Let our lord now command the servants who attend you to look for someone who is skillful in playing the lyre; and when the evil spirit from God is upon you, he will play it, and you will feel better." So Saul said to his servants, "Provide for me someone who can play well, and bring him to me." One of the young men answered, "I have seen a son of Jesse the Bethlehemite who is skillful in playing, a man of valor, a warrior, prudent in speech, and a man of good presence; and the Lord is with him." So Saul sent messengers to Jesse, and said, "Send me your son David who is with the sheep." Jesse took a donkey loaded with bread by his son David to Saul. And David came to Saul, and entered his service. Saul loved him greatly, and he became his armor-bearer. Saul sent to Jesse saying, "Let David remain in my service, for he has found favor in my sight." And whenever the evil spirit from God came upon Saul, David took the lyre and played it with his hand, and Saul would be relieved and feel better, and the evil spirit would depart from him. *(1 Samuel 16:14–23)*

We have known from the beginning, that institutional leadership alone cannot reveal the presence of God. We need artists—musicians, singers, dancers—to bring the energy, life, movement and emotion needed to show authentically the awesome face of God:

So the builders built the temple of the Lord. And the priests stood arrayed in their vestments, with musical instruments and trumpets, and the Levites, the sons of Asaph, with cymbals, praising the LORD and blessing him, according to the directions of King David of Israel; they sang hymns, giving thanks to the LORD, "For his goodness and his glory are forever upon all Israel." And all the people sounded trumpets and shouted with a great shout, praising the LORD for the erection of the house of the LORD. Some of the levitical priests and heads of ancestral houses, old men who had seen the former house, came to the building of this one with outcries and loud weeping, while many came with trumpets and a joyful noise, so that the people could not hear the trumpets because of the weeping of the people. *(1 Esdras 5:58–65)*

It was the duty of the trumpeters and singers to make themselves heard in unison in praise and thanksgiving to the LORD, and when the song was raised, with trumpets and cymbals and other musical instruments, in praise to the LORD,

"For he is good
for his steadfast love endures forever,"

the house, the house of the LORD, was filled with a cloud, so that the priests could not stand to minister because of the cloud; for the glory of the LORD filled the house of God. *(2 Chronicles 5:13–14)*

Music for the ancients was the most honest and right way to express the inexpressible, a language of the heart to say what words alone fail to communicate. They had to sing—they had no choice. God had penetrated their lives too deeply and too powerfully for them to respond in any other way:

David and all Israel were dancing before God with all their might, with song and lyres and harps and tambourines and cymbals and trumpets. *(1 Chronicles 13:8)*

O give thanks to the LORD, call on his name,
make known his deeds among the peoples.
Sing to him, sing praises to him,
tell of all his wonderful works. *(1 Chronicles 16:8–9)*

The songs of their tradition were not enough. They ached and longed to find new ways to express their joy and identity as God's people. There are always new songs to compose, new canticles to sing and fresh melodies to keep the story alive. Composers, take heart, your calling is strong:

O sing to the LORD a new song;
sing to the LORD, all the earth. *(Psalm 96:1)*

Begin a song to my God with tambourines,
sing to my LORD with cymbals.
Raise to him a new psalm,
exalt him, and call upon his name....
I will sing to my God a new song:
O Lord, you are great and glorious,
wonderful in strength, invincible. *(Judith 16:1, 13)*

Let us now sing the praises of...
those who composed musical tunes,
or put verses in writing;...
all these were honored in their generations,
and were the pride of their times....

Their bodies are buried in peace,
  but their name lives on generation after generation.
The assembly declares their wisdom,
  and the congregation proclaims their praise. *(Sirach 44:1,5,7,14–15)*

To sing is not enough, however. We have to live the song. We cannot see the song as an end in itself. As ministers of music, we have to keep pointing beyond ourselves, beyond the music, beyond the words, because while we sing, pain and suffering can be found everywhere. While we sing, the poor and the disenfranchised continue to be trampled upon. While we sing, violence and abuse tear away at our families and communities. While we sing, addiction continues to poison our young people. While we sing, the homeless and hungry cry out for meaning. Our songs mean nothing without intentional and unconditional love, compassion and commitment to bring about justice and peace. Think of the passage from Amos 5 quoted in the previous chapter. Think also of the words of Paul:

If I speak in the tongues of mortals and of angels,
but do not have love, I am a noisy gong or a clanging cymbal. *(1 Corinthians 13:1)*

The liturgy requires music—to have liturgy and have no music is a contradiction in terms. There is no such thing as a "quiet" Mass, or service without song. The beginnings and origins of worship are glued together with song:

I wash my hands in innocence,
  and go around your altar, O Lord,
singing aloud a song of thanksgiving,
  and telling all your wondrous deeds. *(Psalm 26:6–7)*

O come, let us sing to the Lord;
  let us make a joyful noise to the rock of our salvation!
Let us come into his presence with thanksgiving;
  let us make a joyful noise to him with songs of praise! *(Psalm 95:1–2)*

When we feel cut off, God gives us a voice and a melody to express our hurt, our rage and even our anger. Song allows us to go even as far as to shake our fists at God, and with all of our humanity, cry out in wonder, questioning whether or not there is a God that truly cares. Even when we feel we have nothing to sing about, God gives us the notes and the words to feel what we feel, no matter how cynical, no matter how hopeless:

By the rivers of Babylon—
  there we sat down and there we wept
  when we remembered Zion.
On the willows there
  we hung up our harps.
For there our captors
  asked us for songs,

and our tormenters asked for mirth, saying,
   "Sing us one of the songs of Zion!"
How could we sing the LORD's song in a foreign land? *(Psalm 137:1–4)*

Music can break through our loneliness, our desperation and our experience of isolation. We will never be orphaned, for God is with us, intimately, passionately and always by our side. The Hebrew nation knew this well, and their song reminds us that God has never slept, for God is with us, and we are never forgotten:

When the LORD restored the fortunes of Zion,
   we were like those in a dream.
Then our mouth was filled with laughter,
   and our tongue with shouts of joy;
then it was said among the nations,
   "The LORD has done great things for them."
The LORD has done great things for us,
   and we rejoiced....
May those who sow in tears
   reap with shouts of joy.
Those who go out weeping,
   bearing the seed for sowing,
shall come home with shouts of joy,
   carrying their sheaves. *(Psalm 126)*

Sometimes we can't help it—sometimes we are just filled to the brim, for God's power, love and grace is too awesome to contain. We cannot explain why or how. Sometimes we have no other choice except to give praise:

Make a joyful noise to the LORD, all the earth;
   break forth into joyous song and sing praises. *(Psalm 98:4)*

Praise the LORD!
Praise God in his sanctuary;
   praise him in his mighty firmament!
Praise him for his mighty deeds;
   praise him according to his surpassing greatness!

Praise him with trumpet sound;
   praise him with lute and harp!
Praise him with tambourine and dance;
   praise him with strings and pipe!
Praise him with clanging cymbals;
   praise him with loud clashing cymbals!

Let everything that breathes praise the LORD!
Praise the LORD! *(Psalm 150)*

Where love is present, there is singing. When God brings together people in relationship, it is for God's glory. When our hearts are stirring, we will do outrageous things, such as breaking out in song:

My beloved speaks and says to me:
"Arise, my love, my fair one,
    and come away;
for now the winter is past,
    the rain is over and gone.
The flowers appear on the earth;
    the time of singing has come...." *(Song of Solomon 2:10–12)*

There are the sounds of nature, which provide a backdrop for our praise. God's glory is to be found everywhere, and all creation sings for joy in response to God's gentle and lavish care:

You visit the earth and water it,
    you greatly enrich it;
the river of God is full of water;
    you provide the people with grain,
    for so you have prepared it.
You water its furrows abundantly,
    settling its ridges,
softening it with showers,
    and blessing its growth.
You crown the year with your bounty;
    your wagon tracks overflow with richness.
The pastures of the wilderness overflow,
    the hills gird themselves with joy,
the meadows clothe themselves with flocks,
    the valleys deck themselves with grain,
    they shout and sing together for joy. *(Psalm 65:9–13)*

The greatest composition that God gave us, was the music that accompanied the birth of the Messiah. Jesus the "word made flesh." There is no greater gift to sing about:

Glory to God in the highest heaven,
And on earth peace among those whom he favors! *(Luke 2:14)*

Music helps our prayer and longings become real, focused and honest. It is impossible to sing lies before our God:

The Ministry and Mission of Sung Prayer

When you are praying, do not heap up empty phrases…. *(Matthew 6:7)*

Singing has always given people courage. It was that for Jesus, and for his disciples, and has been for all of us who have been listening. When we sing, we can face and embrace the cross as we pound the pilgrim path:

When they had sung the hymn, they went out to the Mount of Olives. *(Mark 14:26)*

About midnight Paul and Silas were praying and singing hymns to God, and the prisoners were listening to them. *(Acts 16:25)*

We do not sing just because it feels good. We sing because it forms us, challenges us and changes us to be better than we are. As music ministers, when we sing, we are our best selves. When we sing, our demons disappear, and our failings are put in perspective. When we sing before God, those sounds cut through the din and noise. We see more clearly and we witness to the truth:

Now, brothers and sisters, if I come to you speaking in tongues, how will I benefit you unless I speak to you in some revelation or knowledge or prophecy or teaching? It is the same way with lifeless instruments that produce sound, such as the flute or the harp. If they do not give distinct notes, how will anyone know what is being played? And if the bugle gives an indistinct sound, who will get ready for battle? So with yourselves; if in a tongue you utter speech that is not intelligible, how will anyone know what is being said? For you will be speaking into the air. There are doubtless many different kinds of sounds in the world, and nothing is without sound. If then I do not know the meaning of a sound, I will be a foreigner to the speaker and the speaker a foreigner to me. So with yourselves; since you are eager for spiritual gifts, strive to excel in them for building up the church. *(1 Corinthians 14:6–12)*

We are called to be a thankful people, and music can help us to be just that. Our songs should be a meditation, a living sign of God's goodness, God's fidelity, God's promise:

It is good to give thanks to the LORD,
    to sing praises to your name, O Most High;
to declare your steadfast love in the morning,
    and your faithfulness by night,
to the music of the lute and the harp,
    to the melody of the lyre.
For you, O LORD, have made me glad by your work;
    at the work of your hands I sing for joy. *(Psalm 92:1–4)*

…be filled with the Spirit, as you sing psalms and hymns and spiritual songs among yourselves, singing and making melody to the Lord in your hearts, giving thanks to God the Father at all times and for everything in the name of our Lord Jesus Christ. *(Ephesians 5:18b–20)*

Let the word of Christ dwell in you richly; teach and admonish one another in all wisdom; and with gratitude in your hearts sing psalms, hymns, and spiritual songs to God. And whatever you do, in word or deed, do everything in the name of the Lord Jesus, giving thanks to God the Father through him. *(Colossians 3:16–17)*

…pray without ceasing, give thanks in all circumstances…. *(1 Thessalonians 5:17–18)*

Music has the ability to correct our thinking about ourselves. It helps us to remember who we are, and who God is. Music in the liturgy and in our communal life of prayer should do just that—celebrate God's presence, connect with the blessings we have been given, and respond with the entirety of our lives. This blending of blessing and mission—this is our destiny. This is what gives us breath to sing:

Day and night without ceasing they sing,
"Holy, holy, holy,
the Lord God the Almighty,
who was and is and is to come." *(Revelation 4:8b)*

And I saw what appeared to be a sea of glass mixed with fire, and those who had conquered the beast and its image and the number of its name, standing beside the sea of glass with harps of God in their hands. And they sing the song of Moses, the servant of God, and the song of the Lamb:
"Great and amazing are your deeds,
Lord God the Almighty!
Just and true are your ways,
King of the nations!
Lord, who will not fear
and glorify your name?
For you alone are holy.
All nations will come
and worship before you,
for your judgments have been revealed." *(Revelation 15:2–4)*

CHAPTER THREE

TOWARD A SPIRITUALITY OF MUSIC MINISTRY

> The purpose of music and text is not merely to affirm widely held values or to invoke participation. The purpose of song in the rite is to provoke a decision (*metanoia*) regarding our commitment to Jesus of Nazareth and to one another. —*Tom Conry*[1]

All of you who are musicians reading this book certainly know and have experienced the power of music. Music, like all art, is a unique language that can express the awe, wonder and the pain of life in ways mere speech fails. We know that music has always been a cornerstone for our understanding of history and various cultures, and its place in the ongoing story of the church is rich with many treasures. Throughout the ages we know that music has been at the heart of human struggle and growth. The spirituals of those in slavery, the songs of pilgrims throughout the world, the laments of those who suffered the Holocaust in our recent memory: This music was, and continues to be, a binding spiritual force for those fighting for civil rights in North America and throughout all corners of the world.

Music continues to be such a force. The emergence of the New Age movement has elevated awareness of music's therapeutic nature to new levels. Different musical expressions (such as rap music, for example) have empowered various groups to claim and celebrate their identity and culture. We know that people find that a song can express their thoughts more clearly than their own words; couples in love speak about "their song," which to them communicates to themselves and others the profound intimacy of their relationship. Music is all around us, even without our permission or request for it. Muzak permeates the waiting rooms of doctors and dentists; it is played relentlessly in elevators and shopping malls. If we have been paying attention, we know that teenagers are more influenced by the Top 40 than they are by the traditional family, educational and church structures. Music can stir our emotions into action. It can calm and center us, it can unify and also divide, and for better or for worse, it can manipulate and shape our thoughts, our beliefs and, yes, even our faith. To not recognize its power and influence is to have our heads in the sand.

Although we as a people participate in making music in our culture and age less and less, until relatively recently, as history and anthropology show us, music was an activity of the common people. The development of musical sophistication in primarily Western culture led to its becoming more and more an activity of the few and skilled. Today, music is actually an activity that often separates and isolates us (for example, think of the way portable radios, cassette and compact disc players, with or without headphones, are commonly used), that emphasizes our individualism, as opposed to our unity. These, and many other dynamics, influence how music can or cannot be experienced as a communal expression of faith in ritual and other settings.

Why have we responded to the call to be ministers of sung prayer under these circumstances? It is certainly not for the great pay, job security, or ongoing affirmation from our pastors or parishioners. Just as many different reasons and motivations bring people to the worship experience, many different reasons call people to be ministers of music. Some folks just plain love to sing. Others love making music with others and are attracted to the communal dimension of singing with a choir or other ensemble in the parish. Some feel called, and yet others feel pressured, or "guilted," into being involved, and there still lurks in parishes the person who needs an audience or place to perform. Regardless of the origins of our involvement, I strongly believe that it is helpful to reflect upon what we are called to be about in the liturgy and all ministerial activity. What follows are ten strands for us to consider as ministers of music.

MUSIC MINISTRY IS A WAY TO EXPRESS GOD'S PRESENCE AMONG US

Liturgical music should always attempt to celebrate, express and name our God, and the many ways God is made known to us. It proclaims the hope, not that God will make things easy for us or that life tomorrow will necessarily be easier, but rather that in whatever life situation we find ourselves, God is with us—God is in the center of all of things. In other words, music ministry proclaims the hope that God *is*. God is worth believing in; there is life in the midst of death; there is hope in the midst of hopelessness; there is truth when there seems to be nothing but lies. We need music to give voice to our desire for, and dependence on, God:

> I want to call you by your name while I live,
> I will call you, "My God,"
> I will thank you,
> I will sing my praise to you.
> God calls to me: "Come forth from your grave."
> Like an eagle, like an eagle I find strength. *(David Haas ©GIA)*[2]

Music also gives voice to our response to the call of God to serve:

> God has chosen me, God has chosen me
> to bring good news to the poor.
> God has chosen me, God has chosen me
> to bring new sight for those searching for light:
> God has chosen me, chosen me.
>
> God has chosen me, God has chosen me,
> to set a-light a new fire.
> God has chosen me, God has chosen me

to bring to birth a new kingdom on earth:
God has chosen me, chosen me.

God is calling me, God is calling me
in all whose cry is unheard.
God is calling me, God is calling me
to raise up the voice with no power or choice:
God is calling me, calling me:

And to tell the world that God's kingdom is near,
to remove oppression and break down fear,
yes, God's time is near, God's time is near. [3]

We sing of a God who continually surprises and awes us by unconditional love and forgiveness, far beyond what our dreams could ever imagine:

O my soul: bless the Lord,
Forgiving our offenses, healing all our ills!
O my soul: I will bless the Lord,
Who redeems us from destruction, and crowns us with compassion!

Merciful and gracious;
Our God is slow to anger, abounding in love!
Our tender God will not haunt us with our sins;
No longer abandoned! Our God is here to save us!

As the east is from the west,
God will come and cast away all guilt and shame!
With tenderness, and parents to their children,
Healing and compassion for those who fear the Lord! *(David Haas ©GIA)*[4]

And of course, we need songs to express our hope in the promise of God's realm, and to keep us strong as we pound the pilgrim path:

I will not die before I've lived to see that land;
firm as the earth, your own promise.
I'll not let go until I've held it in my hand;
that word of hope, and gentle laughter.

I will not rest until your dawn is in my eyes;
that fragile light, new like morning.
I will not sleep before I've wakened to that sunrise,
And all the world knows your glory.

And I will breathe in that mighty wind of justice;
I'll know my name and rise up singing.
And I will call until my words bring on the thunder;
Washed in that rain, then I'll know you.

You will stand up for the poor and the needy;
You'll break the chains that bind your people.
For you are home for the lost and the desperate;
Your strong right hand goes before us.

For your right hand has delivered us from death;
You have regarded our tears,
You who are goodness and grace.[5]

MUSIC MINISTRY IS ABOUT EMPOWERING RITUAL AND SERVING THE WORSHIP OF GOD'S PEOPLE

Music ministers must always remember that regardless of the beauty or power of a particular piece of music, in the context of liturgy, it always serves the ritual event. All too often people experience music as an appendage to liturgy. I cannot begin to count the number of times I have heard someone say, "I come to Mass to pray, *not* sing." There are at least a couple of reasons for this way of thinking. First, many of the people who express these sentiments were *taught* that they were not to participate in singing. Singing was the job of the choir or schola. Second, often music is inserted into the liturgy and implemented without skill.

Part of the problem is that we music ministers usually became musicians first and are not necessarily knowledgeable and skilled in liturgy. We need to become more than just good musicians. We need to read about the liturgy, to study and know the documentation and become skilled in the art of ritual music, not music that serves as a sort of intermission, or scene-change music, or inspirational entertainment.

We have in the past often considered music in church as filler, something to accompany and take care of long and sometimes awkward moments. This developed into what is popularly known as the Four Hymn-Syndrome. We sing to get the priest down the aisle (entrance hymn); we need music to bring up the gifts and take up the collection (the offertory hymn). Then, there is music to accompany the procession of the Communion lines (the Communion hymn) and to accompany the priest out of the sanctuary down the aisle again (the recessional hymn). In the Four Hymn-Syndrome, music serves as filler. Our Protestant brothers and sisters are appalled that we often sing only two or three stanzas of a hymn, instead of singing the hymn in its entirety.

We need to move from an understanding of music as filler to an understanding of *ritual* music. In other words, there is a great difference between *singing at* the liturgy and *singing* the liturgy. Music is the very language in which we pray the liturgy. When ritual music is at its best, communal worship is *sung*, it is *repetitive* and it is done *by heart*. Ritual music does not and cannot tolerate having an audience. It is to be sung and prayed by *all*, not by a select few. Although occasional experiences of a solo selection or choir anthem are not to be prohibited, these are not at the heart of our ministry of music and should never dominate our energies or priorities.

We need to learn about the liturgy, about ritual forms, such as acclamations, litanies and intercessory prayer, about dialogic forms and mantras, as well as about responsorial singing and strophic hymnody. We should study the various rhythms of ritual, come to know the high and low points in the various ritual units and understand proper creativity and adaptation.

Music serves ritual prayer. It should go without saying that an important role of music in liturgy is to serve the prayer of the gathered assembly. While music can serve to inspire or draw people into individual contemplation, its primary responsibility is to help serve the *communal* prayer of the assembly.

MUSIC MINISTRY IS ABOUT INTENSIFYING THE SYMBOLIC

Symbols are signs, actions and gestures that attempt to express what we believe. They foster and nurture the very center of what we value. The liturgy by its very essence is symbolic, with particular symbols that strive to name that which is unnamable:

> While our words and art forms cannot contain or confine God, they can, like the world itself, be icons, avenues of approach, numinous presences, ways of touching without totally grasping or seizing. Flood, fire, the rock, the sea, the mountain, the cloud, the political situations and institutions of succeeding periods—in all of them Israel touched the face of God, found help for discerning a way, moved toward the reign of justice and peace. [6]

It can be said that our artful expressions help serve as "avenues of approach," and music lies before us as a pathway to entering into the mystery of God, the mystery of life and death. Our life then has meaning as a result of suffering and the journey toward new life. We speak and use the symbolic language of music to sojourn to a new place, a new way of living, to the biblical vision of God's way:

> Then I saw a new heaven and a new earth; for the first heaven and the first earth had passed away, and the sea was no more. And I saw the holy city, the new Jerusalem, coming down out of heaven from God, prepared as a bride adorned for her husband. And I heard a loud voice from the throne saying,
>
>> "See, the home of God is among mortals.
>> He will dwell with them as their God;
>> they will be his peoples,
>> and God himself will be with them;
>> he will wipe every tear from their eyes.
>> Death will be no more;

mourning and crying and pain will be no more,
for the first things have passed away.
And the one who was seated on the throne said, "See, I am making all things new."
(Revelation 21:1–5a)

Music ministry enables all seekers to rejoice and revel in this promise. We need to recognize and be humbled by the seductive power of sound as symbolic language in ritual activity:

> Music is a part of the symbolic nature of worship. Music's sacramental power is rooted in the nature of sound, the raw materials for music. Sound itself is our starting point for understanding music and its capacity to serve as a vehicle for God's self-revelation. Sound's temporality, for example, symbolizes a God active in creation and history; its seemingly insubstantial nature symbolizes God who is both present and hidden; its dynamism symbolizes a God who calls us into dialogue; its ability to unify symbolizes our union with God and others; its evocation of personal presence symbolizes a God who we perceive as personal.[7]

When we take this statement of music's power to heart, we recognize that music has a potential to express the vast landscape of the human condition and our relationship to God, and our need for God. This expression finds richness in our liturgical tradition, which is a language of symbols. Symbols are the storehouse of our beliefs, and these beliefs have the potential to be the most powerful force in the world. As ministers of music, we need to dig deep into the many genres, forms and styles that can echo and ratify the reality of God's action in our lives.

MUSIC MINISTRY IS FORMATIONAL: EVANGELIZING, CATECHIZING, CELEBRATING AND BUILDING UP THE BODY OF CHRIST

Music ministry is always *formational*. This is different from saying that in worship, music "teaches." While we can certainly learn much from our sung prayer, effective music ministry forms and nurtures the whole person in every aspect of our lives. Music evangelizes because the liturgy is a proclamation of God's vision; music announces and celebrates this vision. It catechizes through its seductive message and pedagogy, and it intensifies our theology and belief within the sinews of our entire selves. The best liturgical music is never didactic; rather, it is metaphorical. It involves the mind, the heart and the soul. Quality worship music should take us over and be corrective, as we attempt to express our faith and beliefs. In communal ritual, music builds up the Body of Christ, because when the Christian assembly together sings both their praise and lament, they bond themselves to one another, and thus are strengthened and empowered to go forth and live the gospel call.

A central point of all ministry is to empower and nurture conversion, whether it be an initial conversion or turning point, or the ongoing conversion (being born again, again and again), for all the baptized. Our hope is all we have, and music ministry and liturgical prayer is always about proclaiming the promise that awaits us on the other side:

We shall rise again on the last day
with the faithful, rich and poor.
Coming to the house of Lord Jesus,
we will find an open door there,
we will find an open door. *(Jeremey Young ©GIA)*[8]

Music is one of the most powerful ways in which we are formed in the Word of God and, as a result, helps praying congregations to reclaim the Scriptures as a cornerstone of their faith life. I would propose that biblically-based liturgical musical compositions have been a primary vehicle for Catholics to rediscover the Bible. How many people in our congregations could stand up and recite from memory Psalm 91? Yet, how many people could sing all of the verses to "On Eagle's Wings" with no music or text in front of them? In other words, liturgical music has been a potent force in how our faith has been "caught" by our communities. How many people remember the homily more clearly than the music sung at a liturgy? The music we sing and pray with on Sunday is highly influential in the lives of believers inside, as well as outside, the worship environment.

MUSIC MINISTRY IS PROPHETIC, BREAKING OPEN NEW IMAGES OF GOD AND THE CHURCH

Arguably, one of the most groundbreaking documents that exploded from the Second Vatican Council was *The Constitution on the Church* (also known as *Lumen Gentium*). Throughout, this document calls the church "the People of God" and speaks repeatedly of the mission that belongs and is given to all of us, not just to a selected few leaders. For many Catholics this is still new. It is our baptism that calls us to ministry, not ordination. The Scriptures give us a clear foundation for this identity, this most awesome gift from God:

> The days are surely coming, says the LORD, when I will make a new covenant with the house of Israel and the house of Judah....I will put my law within them, and I will write it on their hearts; and I will be their God, and they shall be my people. No longer shall they teach one another, or say to one another, "Know the LORD," for they shall all know me from the least of them to the greatest, says the LORD. *(Jeremiah 31:31–34)*

> So then you are no longer strangers and aliens, but you are citizens with the saints and also members of the household of God...with Christ Jesus himself as the cornerstone....in whom you also are built together spiritually into a dwelling place for God. *(Ephesians 2:19–22)*

> ...you are a chosen race, a royal priesthood, a holy nation, God's own people....
> Once you were not a people,
> but now you are God's people. *(1 Peter 2:9–10)*

When we take the time to reflect on these passages (and many other passages like them), we should feel humbled and filled with awe that God holds us in this esteem. Liturgy and the ritual music wedded to it are critical for the Christian community to revel in, understand and live out this gift and promise, for it is in the celebration of liturgy that we have our foundations of theology and our most profound expression of the Christian story. If we believe that music is intrinsic to liturgy, the implications for us charged with music ministry are profound:

> Christian ritual music, as a sacramental event, expresses and shapes our image of God. Many factors come together in the musical event, and each of these contributes to the expressive and creative quality of music. Texts, musical forms, styles of musical leadership, and even the technology employed in our ritual music making express and shape our faith. They are, therefore, foundational lents in the church's first theology, the liturgy. Appreciating the theological import of the various facets of Christian ritual music is, thus, an essential task in the forging of our sung worship.[9]

While ministers of music do not need to have a degree in theology or religious studies, they need to accept the responsibility of the message and vision of church that is expressed in the music chosen for worship. The language found in our musical selections can both proclaim or misrepresent and destroy the message. The truth is that we live in a culture in which individualism is rampant. The focus is on the individual. It is this message of individual salvation that sometimes overwhelms and harms the more authentic communal aspect of liturgy. We must be careful not to engage ourselves in pieces of sacred music that are narcissistic, self-indulgent or overtly sentimental. This is where the issue of inclusive language must be addressed. Great sensitivity is needed when some are alienated (whether or not it is intended) in the words and images prayed and sung.

Music (as well as all of the gifts employed in worship) has the ability to proclaim new images, new expressions and fresh approaches as we journey as a community of faith. The following two liturgical music texts beautifully express who the church really is:

I myself am the bread of life.
You and I are the bread of life,
taken and blessed, broken and shared by Christ
that the world might live.

This bread is spirit, gift of the Maker's love,
and we who share it know that we can be one:
a living sign of God in Christ.

Here is God's kingdom given to us as food.
This is our body, this is our blood:
a living sign of God in Christ.

Lives broken open, stories shared aloud,
become a banquet, a shelter for the world:
a living sign of God in Christ.[10]

We are God's chosen people,
we are the saints.
We are God's work of art
signed and set apart. Let us sing![11]

It is also very important that we free our communities from some of the solitary and limiting understandings of who God is. God is certainly beyond our words, but as Christian believers, we have always needed to grasp and have attempted to name more deeply the essence of God and the galaxy of personalities and qualities of God.

God is more than a divine power and ruler, but also the grand designer and healer of all in creation that lives and breathes:

Love that sends the rivers dancing,
love that waters all that lives,
love that heals and holds
and rouses and forgives.
You are food for all your creatures,
you are hunger in the soul,
in your hands the broken hearted are made whole. *(Marty Haugen ©GIA)*[12]

God is one whom we have known to walk with us, to share our form and to be the mirror of all we are called to be:

God beyond all names, you have made us in your image;
we are like you, we reflect you; we are woman, we are man.

God beyond all words, all creation tells your story;
you have shaken with our laughter, you have trembled with our tears.

All around us we have known you,
all creation lives to hold you,
In our living and our dying we are bringing you to birth.[13]

God is known and proclaimed in the presence of those who answer the call to be people of compassion, mercy and courage:

Who stands in the storm like a beacon,
with hope for the ravaged and weakened?
Whose presence is healing for young and for old,
to friend and to stranger the same?
This is my servant, whom I shall uphold,
his name is Christ is her name![14]

God is everywhere, in all that is beautiful, in all the wonders of creation. God's bountiful energy is our spur to meditate and act:

God of the ocean and sea!
Bathe us anew with wisdom from heaven.
Rivers and life flowing streams!
Call us again to be living water,
Flooding and filling the earth with new life!

God of the wind and the breeze!
Breathe in our hearts the spirit of Jesus.
Voice and the presence of God!
Guide us to hear the call of creation,
Singing and dancing the cry of delight!

God of the forests and trees!
Color our lives with love and compassion.
Source of all beauty and truth!
Help us to live as shade for the weary,
Hope for the broken and hope for the lost!

God of the morning and night!
Gift all our days with signs of your promise.
Sunlight and darkness are yours!
In death and life, may we know your rising,
Alpha, Omega, beginning and end!

God of the planets and stars!
Power our dreams and lift us to glory.
Jesus, the light of the world!
Shine in our lives and be "God among us,"
Building your kingdom, the city of peace! *(David Haas ©GIA)*[15]

God is awesome mystery, filled with contradictions and patterns great and powerful, most of the time beyond our understanding:

You have passed by, you came like fire that lights the skies,
sparks falling from your name glow in our hearts like eyes.
In tatters hangs your word, draped round our world and torn;
now we shall live in you; like clothing you are worn.[16]

God is the one for whom we all seek, in whom we find our hope, the one who knows us well, even more than we know ourselves, and in whom we always find acceptance, light, peace and love:

…You held me at my birth,
You sang my name, were glad to see my face
You are my sky, my shining sun,
and in your love there's always room
to be, and grow, yet find a home,
a settled place.[17]

MUSIC MINISTRY RAISES MORE QUESTIONS THAN ANSWERS

While ministry should certainly be about revealing the presence and assurance of God's activity in our lives, it also should be about asking questions and probing the issues that are necessary for our lives. Jesus' teaching and ministry constantly confused and baffled his disciples. He was always forcing the questions and challenging presumptions in a way that could lead to authentic and honest faith and hope. The Scriptures are filled with questions and moments of puzzlement that become the opportunity for the mystery of God to be revealed. Consider some of the questions that the New Testament puts in front of us:

"Who then is this, that even the wind and the sea obey him?" *(Mark 4:41b)*

"Why do you look for the living among the dead?" *(Luke 24:5)*

Questions abound in the walk of faith and our music should not try to ignore these ambiguities; rather, our music should reflect upon and even celebrate these questions and doubts. If we really believe that our prayer and music can definitively name, know and contain who God is, how God acts in our lives and what God's motives are, then we are not giving our people a "thick slice" of who God is, and we are in danger of heresy:

Who are you God, where do you live?
High in the mountains, deep in the ocean, are you the wind?

Are you the rain, or the roar of the sea?
Spinner of chaos, breathing and stirring deep within?

Fire of love, healer of tears,
Friend of the lonely, bread for the hungry, hope for the poor!

Dancer of life, mystery of death;
Giver and taker, loving creator, guiding light!

You, our desire, maker of dreams;
Voice of the trumpet, author of silence, blossom of truth!

Wonder of strength, compassion and calm,
Singer of mercy, source of our safety; justice and peace!

All of your ways are here in our midst:
Presence and absence, laughter and anger; life and death!

What is your name? How are you known?
Mother or Father? Sister or Brother? You are God—beyond our words! *(David Haas ©GIA)*[18]

Responsible music in our prayer should both rearticulate the questions in the stories of the Scriptures and challenge us to ask new questions:

How shall I sing to God,
When life is filled with gladness,
loving and birth,
wonder and worth?
I'll sing from the heart,
thankfully receiving,
joyful in believing,
This is my song, I'll sing it with love.

How shall I sing to God
when life is filled with bleakness,
empty and chill,
breaking my will?
I'll sing through my pain,
angrily or aching,
crying or complaining.
This is my song, I'll sing it with love.

How shall I sing to God
and tell my Savior's story:
Passover bread,
life from the dead?
I'll sing with my life,
witnessing and giving,
risking and forgiving.
This is my song, I'll sing it with love.[19]

In all of this, good music ministry enables all who believe to express their faith *and* doubt in the midst of the totality of life.

MUSIC MINISTRY IS ABOUT TELLING THE TRUTH

As we have seen, we believers often live not with absolute assurance but rather, in hope. We often experience a God who is far away and seems inattentive. If we were to be truthful in our sung prayer and articulate honestly the experience of many people, we probably would sing: "... I *don't* know you are near." An important (but often silent or stifled) aspect of our faith is struggling with broken promises and the need to raise our voices in honest anger and lament:

> Where can we find you, are you absent?
> Is your promise one that we can cling to?
> We scream in hope to hear your voice,
> And once again we risk the call to find you!
> Are you present in this place?
> We long for you O God, show us your face! *(David Haas ©GIA)*[20]

> My God, my God, why have you forsaken me? *(Psalm 22:1)*

Sung prayer can celebrate the journey of waiting and hoping even when it is much easier to be cynical and suspect:

> Full of your presence and full of your absence.
>   I wait,
> All my life long if I must,
> And I do not care who knows it.[21]

When we sing, we should not lie. Sung prayer can give us the power to confront the work we have yet to accomplish as God's people. It needs to tell the truth, and in the midst of that truth, call us to conversion and action:

> Still the nations curse the darkness, still the rich oppress the poor;
> Still the earth is bruised and broken by the ones who still want more.
> Come and wake us from our sleeping, so our hearts cannot ignore
> All your people lost and broken, all your children at our door.

> Show us Christ in one another, make us servants strong and true;
> Give us all your love of justice so we do what you would do.
> Let us call all people holy, let us pledge our lives anew,
> Make us one with all the lowly, let us all be one in you. *(Marty Haugen ©GIA)*[22]

Songs and hymns can have a way of reminding us of who we are. It is God who is in charge. We must remember that we are mortal, and that we know not the day or hour when the fragility and finite nature of our existence will confront us:

Steal away, steal away,
Steal away to Jesus.
Steal away, steal away home.
I ain't got long to stay here.[23]

MUSIC MINISTRY (AND ALL MINISTRY) IS GROUNDED IN RELATIONSHIPS: IN COMMUNITY, AND IN MAKING, NURTURING AND SOLIDIFYING CONNECTIONS

If we do not live in relationship with people and with God's creation, I believe that we are in danger of not breathing. It is in relationship that we most profoundly encounter the presence of God.

My dear friends from Hawaii have taught me much about this. In traditional Hawaiian mythology and spirituality, we find the deepest understanding of their word *Aloha*. The important part of the word is the "ha" at the end. The "ha" means "the breath of life." When native Hawaiian people greet each other, an intimate embrace accompanies the "aloha" greeting, never a distant handshake. When they embrace they often exchange their breath through their nostrils, as a sign of the exchange of the divine breath, the "breath of life," that is deep within them. The island people there have another word: *ha'ole*. This word in recent years has come to identify someone who is from "far away." But the original meaning of "ha'ole" designated someone who wanted to keep their distance, who wanted to shake hands rather than embrace, who wanted to remain detached in sharing with others—in other words, someone who refused to share the "breath of life."

If we are called to ministry, we are called to share this "breath of life" with each other. Music ministry should be an expression of our common stories, our common walk with each other, our common dependence on the power of God in our lives. This commonality will be evident beyond tabernacles, church buildings or sacred objects. It is also found in the lives and presence of those around us. We need to share the breath of life with each other, to have hope in the people of God or else we will wander hopelessly into the abyss of a "half-alive" existence. We desperately need music that will name, encourage and deepen our bonds with each other:

We come to share our story,
we come to break the bread,
we come to know our rising from the dead. *(David Haas ©GIA)*[24]

The story in Luke's Gospel of the two disciples on the road to Emmaus puts this into clear perspective: If we do not live in relationship and welcome the stranger, we are denying ourselves an encounter with the risen Lord. This illustrates one of the important metaphors of the Eucharist: recognizing the mystery of the presence of God, not limiting that presence to the physical presence of the bread and wine only, but including, rather, the full *communal* action of taking, blessing, breaking and sharing the bread together. In these actions we proclaim the reality that we are for each other, and that for which we long:

In the breaking of bread
we have known him;
we have been fed.
Jesus the stranger,
Jesus the Lord,
be our companion;
be our hope.[25]

MUSIC MINISTRY IS PASTORAL CARE

People come to prayer often bringing the deepest pains and hurts of their existence. The average person in the pew is not concerned with the "liturgical correctness" of our musical and liturgical choices, our picking the right responsorial psalm, making sure the choir sings in tune or whether or not the guitarist has the capo on the right fret. Most people coming to worship could care less about these things, with which we music ministers are far too often obsessed. Most people are concerned about their children and how they will put food on the table. Most are concerned with how to cope when someone close to them has just been diagnosed with AIDS. Most people are dealing with the realities of the loss of their job, the breaking up of a relationship, living with an addiction—in other words, the real "stuff" of life.

If our ministry of music is not concerned with these things, that is, the real lives of people, then our ministry should be damned. While liturgy is not a therapy session, our common prayer should give hope to people who believe that there is a God who loves them and will not leave them abandoned in the midst of the struggles of life. Good liturgy proclaims life in the midst of death, hope in a world of hopelessness, happiness and peace in the presence of pain and fear. Music has the ability to reach out, touch and provide a source of healing. In the context of liturgy, music should always proclaim Jesus, the Anointed One who healed the blind man, the Christ who forgave and dined with sinners and the Messiah who gave freedom to those who were trapped by their slavery:

Do not be afraid, I am with you,
I have called you each by name.
Come and follow me,
I will bring you home.
I love you and you are mine. *(David Haas ©GIA)*[26]

And he will raise you up on eagle's wings,
bear you on the breath of dawn,
make you to shine like the sun,
and hold you in the palm of his hand.[27]

MUSIC MINISTRY IS ABOUT MISSION FOR THE REIGN OF GOD

The central issue of this strand is baptism. One way to describe the Christian life is to say that our entire life is to be spent figuring out what our baptism means. For those awaiting initiation into the church, the consuming goal should be to focus on what will be asked of them because of their baptism. Baptism is about preparing and committing ourselves to be missionaries. Music ministry should be about giving us a voice and tools in which we can express and deepen our zeal for Jesus Christ and for the reign of God. Music ministry should be forever pushing the edges to challenge believers not to be satisfied with the present condition. It should proclaim hope in the promise of God and send us all forth to do the work of building the city of God. This promise of God demands a life response from us, a commitment in terms of our discipleship:

> We are called to act with justice,
> we are called to love tenderly,
> we are called to serve one another,
> and walk humbly with God! *(David Haas ©GIA)*[28]

If our liturgy, including the music we pray with, is not about justice and mission, then it is a false enterprise and anti-gospel. Music ministry, and the entire liturgy, form a "dismissal." This dismissal is not to the parking lot, but to the streets, to the AIDS hospice, to the nursing home, to the prisons and schools, to the poor and the hungry, the lonely and disenfranchised, to all of us who are in need of good news. We sing to bring forth the new and eternal Jerusalem:

> In days to come the desert shall bloom. Rivers will run there,
>   soon, very soon.
> So what shall we fear, though death do its worst?
> The word of our God is the last shall be first, the last shall be first.
>
> Comfort each other, for pain soon must end. A day comes when
>   lion and lamb shall be friends.
> The sightless shall see then, the speechless sing songs.
> The name of our God is the righter of wrongs, the righter of wrongs.
>
> A curtain of fear is being torn down. Prisons are opened; the lost
>   have been found.
> So go tell the seeker what we've seen and heard:
> The name of our God is the keeper of word, the keeper of word.
>
> The streets of Soweto, the docks at Gdansk, Tiannamen Square,
>   the slums of the Bronx,
> When we stand together to stand against hell,
> The name of this people is "Emmanuel," is "Emmanuel."

Close as tomorrow, the sun shall appear.
Freedom is coming, and healing is near.
And I shall be with you in laughter and pain
To stand in the wind and walk in the reign,
To walk in the reign. *(Rory Cooney ©GIA)*[29]

NOTES

[1] Tom Conry, "Calling the Question: Toward a Revisionist Theology of Liturgical Music and Text," *Pastoral Music,* October/November 1983, p. 53.

[2] David Haas, "I Want to Call You," copyright ©1989, GIA Publications. All rights reserved.

[3] Bernadette Farrell, "God Has Chosen Me," copyright ©1990, Bernadette Farrell. Published by OCP Publications. All rights reserved.

[4] David Haas, "Deep Down I Know," copyright ©1993, GIA Publications. All rights reserved.

[5] Tom Conry, "I Will Not Die," copyright ©1984, 1990, TEAM Publications. Published by OCP Publications. All rights reserved.

[6] *Environment and Art in Catholic Worship*, Bishops' Committee on the Liturgy, United States Conference of Catholic Bishops, n. 2.

[7] *The Milwaukee Symposia for Church Composers: A Ten Year Report,* (Portland, Ore.: The Pastoral Press, 1992), 13.

[8] Jeremey Young, "We Shall Rise Again," copyright ©1987, GIA Publications. All rights reserved.

[9] *The Milwaukee Symposia for Church Composers: A Ten Year Report,* 17.

[10] Rory Cooney, "Bread of Life," copyright ©1987, NALR. Published by OCP Publications. All rights reserved.

[11] Rory Cooney, "Song of the Chosen," copyright ©1984, Rory Cooney. Published by OCP Publications. All rights reserved.

[12] Marty Haugen, "Spirit Blowing Through Creation," copyright ©1987, GIA Publications. All rights reserved.

[13] Bernadette Farrell, "God Beyond All Names," copyright ©1990, Bernadette Farrell. Published by OCP Publications. All rights reserved.

[14] Rory Cooney, "Servant Song," copyright ©1987, NALR. Published by OCP Publications. All rights reserved.

[15] David Haas, "God of All Creation," copyright ©1988, GIA Publications. All rights reserved.

[16] Huub Oosterhuis, "Song to Jesus Christ," copyright ©1972, 1984, Gooi en Sticht, bv Baarn, The Netherlands. Published by OCP Publications. All rights reserved.

[17] Brian Wren, "Dear Mother God," copyright ©1994, Hope Publishing Company. All rights reserved.

[18] David Haas, "What Is Your Name," copyright ©1991, GIA Publications. All rights reserved.

[19] Brian Wren, text, "How Shall I Sing to God?" copyright ©1986, Hope Publishing Company. All rights reserved.

[20] David Haas, "We Have Seen and We Have Heard," copyright ©1991, GIA Publications. All rights reserved.

[21] Huub Oosterhuis, text, "You," copyright ©1973, Gooi en Sticht, bv Baarn, The Netherlands. All rights reserved. Exclusive agent for English-language countries: OCP Publications.

[22] Marty Haugen, "God of Day and God of Darkness," copyright ©1985, 1994, GIA Publications. All rights reserved.

[23] "Steal Away," Spiritual.

[24] David Haas, "Song of the Body of Christ," copyright ©1989, GIA Publications. All rights reserved.

[25] Bob Hurd, "In the Breaking of the Bread," copyright ©1984, Bob Hurd. Published by OCP Publications. All rights reserved.

[26] David Haas, "You Are Mine," copyright ©1991, GIA Publications. All rights reserved.

[27] Michael Joncas, "On Eagle's Wings," copyright ©1979, New Dawn Music. Published by OCP Publications. All rights reserved.

[28] David Haas, "We Are Called," copyright ©1988, GIA Publications. All rights reserved.

[29] Rory Cooney, "Walk in the Reign," copyright ©1990, GIA Publications. All rights reserved.

CHAPTER FOUR

*W*HO ARE THE MUSIC MINISTERS?

Since love is Lord of heaven and earth,
how can I keep from singing? —*Traditional Quaker Hymn*

IN LIGHT OF THE SPIRITUALITY issues raised in the previous chapter, we are led to examine the various roles in a parish music ministry that can best empower and implement this vision.

THE MINISTRIES OF MUSIC

THE ASSEMBLY

The assembly as minister may seem like a strange image, still new and hard for many to see. For much of our history as Roman Catholics, the notion of the assembly was not even recognized. They were the "congregation." Their role was to be passive and to be the recipients of the "ministry" given to them by the leaders, who were primarily the priests. The choirs did the singing, not the community. As a result of the liturgical renewal of Vatican II, the more authentic tradition from our history has been restored— that the liturgy is an action of the assembly, and thus, its music is rooted in the assembly as well.

The worship of Christians should never be viewed as something existing primarily in liturgical books, rubrics, rules and documents. We must always be mindful and stay centered on the truth that liturgy is always, without exception, an activity of people. If there is no gathering of people, there is no liturgy. The primary symbol of any liturgical celebration can never be reduced to objects, such as bread, wine, candles, oil or incense. *The Constitution on the Sacred Liturgy* contains one of the most important reference points for this discussion. It demands that "the faithful should be led to that full, conscious, and active participation in liturgical celebrations which is demanded by the very nature of liturgy" (n. 14).

In regard to liturgical song and chant, the mandate is clear:

Bishops and other pastors of souls must take great care to ensure that whenever the sacred action is to be accompanied by chant, the whole body of the faithful may be able to contribute to that active participation which is rightly theirs....[1]

Even though many parishes may find themselves far from reaching these goals, music ministers need to remember that their particular role is supportive. The *primary* minister of music in any liturgical celebration is always a musically untrained assembly.

THE PRESIDING PRIEST

The presiding priest convenes the assembly; is the primary leader of prayer and possesses a unique and critical role as a music minister as well. The presider exercises this ministry of music when leading the ministerial chants or proclaiming the Eucharistic Prayer in sung form. More importantly, however, the presider is seen by the assembly as one of *them*, committed to *their* participation through visual and passionate leadership in the singing of the hymns and acclamations. The priest does not have to possess a fabulous voice, but if the presider is not singing robustly, the assembly will be weakened. The presider gives "order" (thus the term "Holy Orders") to the worship, and models the behavior actively for all who have gathered:

> No other single factor affects the liturgy as much as the attitude, style, and bearing of the celebrant: his sincere faith and warmth as he welcomes the worshipping community; his human naturalness combined with dignity and seriousness as he breaks the Bread of Word and Eucharist.[2]

The presider is first a member of the assembly, and serves (as do all of the ministers) within the assembly. A strong and passionate singing presider is a sign that music is not an appendage to the liturgy, but the very language that is integral and necessary for worship. The presider supports the other ministers of music, and, of course, the other members of the music ministry support and uphold this unique role. The enthusiasm and attentiveness of the presider in the musical settings of the Eucharistic Prayer and other chants unique to the presidential role only enhance and proclaim this joint enterprise.

THE CANTOR

Since Vatican II, arguably the most unique restoration in the musical ministries has been that of the role of the cantor. The earliest traces of this ministry are to be found in the synagogue, with a person who emerged as a volunteer leader of prayer, or "messenger of the people."[3] The integral role of the cantor can best be experienced in a synagogue even today. For early Judaism, and even early Christianity, there was practically no distinction between recited and sung speech in the exercise of worship. Even the Torah (the Scriptures) was known to be cantillated in some form. Because of these roots in Judaism, the earliest cantors in Christian worship settings proclaimed the psalms in sung form.

Throughout the history of the church, the role of the cantor has evolved, changed and even disappeared at times. The recent liturgical renewal has helped us to rediscover the importance of this role, and especially in terms of the role of "psalmist," the singer and proclaimer of the psalms. While the roles of the cantor and the psalmist are at times seen separately, very frequently they are the same person. The role of cantor is finally emerging from its "second-best" status, tolerated only when there is no choir, and now is beginning to be considered as a ministerial key for the sung prayer of the community:

> Among music ministers, the cantor has come to be recognized as having a crucial role in the development of congregational singing. Besides being qualified to lead singing, he or she must have the skills to introduce and teach new music, and to encourage the assembly.[4]

The ministry of the cantor is much like that of the presider, being a leader of prayer and a minister in the best sense of the word. There is a tight balance that cantors have to maintain—while good quality singing is desired and important, this ministry is not one of solo performance and self-attention. The person in this role must obviously have some gift of singing, but one's vocal prowess should not overwhelm the memory of a particular celebration. This balance between leading the singing and dominating the singing is very difficult to achieve. Sometimes, in an effort to not overpower the assembly or draw too much attention to oneself, the cantor may appear to apologize or become "wimpy" in leadership style and direction.

So how important is the cantor? The ministry of cantor (now hang on to your hat) is more important than the ministry of the organist, choir or the ensemble. We often hear people say, "We don't need a cantor at this Mass because we have a choir." To the contrary, celebrations with a choir often need the cantor even more because in those settings the assembly sometimes sees the presence of a choir as permission to sit back, listen and observe. The cantor is the vital link or liaison between the assembly and the leadership in the sanctuary. In parish music programs, the development of a good cantor program and ongoing formation should be at the top of the list of priorities.

Many diocesan liturgy offices and other liturgical organizations sponsor workshops and institutes for cantors. There are also good audio, video and printed resources available. It is always important for cantors to work on their vocal skills and stay attentive to their vocal health. Parishes should invest well in their cantors by sponsoring their attendance at workshops and helping to pay the cost of voice lessons. Our assemblies and our worship deserve such an investment.

THE CHOIR (OR VOCAL ENSEMBLE)

As the role of the cantor emerged strongly from the liturgical reforms of Vatican II, the role of the choir became a problem for many parishes. With a continual and unrelenting emphasis on congregational singing, and with liturgy in the vernacular becoming commonplace, the choir in many communities went through an identity crisis, and in many places, unfortunately, these choirs disintegrated. Many continued to limp along, at best, during those first years following the Council, and the importance of assembly-based singing for some seemed to take the form of a direct attack on choirs. Some choirs to this day still feel their existence is threatened. Also, a new crew of musicians appeared with guitars and tambourines and claimed to be a new voice of liturgical music and, again unfortunately, edged out the so-called "traditional" choir in many instances. The sad development in all of this was and still is that *what kind or style* of music has often become more important than the whole issue of *why* we sing.

Things have been turbulent for the choir, but as a result a more exciting and challenging role has evolved. The choir is an ensemble, whether it be the so-called traditional soprano-alto-tenor-bass (SATB) choir, the folk or contemporary ensemble, the children's choir or the small trio or schola. The choir remains a group of singers, but their mission has expanded. They no longer are to perform for a passive audience; they are members of the assembly who lead people in prayer through their musical gifts. Their charge is to add fire and energy to the worship of the people, and assist through the harmonies and interpretation in their choral singing. They have an important role in helping the assembly to respond robustly in the acclamations, litanies, psalms and hymns. There are also times (which are rare) when it would be appropriate for them to sing an anthem or selection alone.

A true conversion has yet to take place for many choirs. Their role and ministry is not determined by a particular musical style, or by their competence or abilities. Their posture and activity is determined by the liturgy, and is in service to the liturgy. The focus of the choir should not be on repertoire, but rather on *role*. This is where much of the crisis lies in regard to sung prayer: We often pay too much attention to choices in the repertoire, while we neglect to develop and reflect upon a theology of sung prayer.

It has already been noted that since Vatican II many different types of choirs make up the parish music ministry. Some parishes claim two or three different choirs or contemporary ensembles, children's choirs, youth choirs and many other kinds of ensembles. There still exists in some parishes an unhealthy rivalry and competition between these groups, who are often groping for first-class status. While not as prevalent as in the recent past, these tendencies still exist, and the result can endanger a parish's music ministry and the parish at large. In many more parishes, the different ensembles dialogue well with each other, sharing common repertoire (especially in ritual music and acclamations) and uniting with each other for major celebrations and feasts, such as Christmas and Easter. These are healthy signs that the common prayer of the community reigns above taste, style and personal issues.

Choirs need to embrace a role that might be more hidden, yet critically important in its contribution to the liturgy and to the community at large. Beyond their obvious musical and leadership role, the choir is called to community, to be "church," to become an intentional, small Christian community that nurtures and challenges each other in the faith journey.

However, choirs need to be open circles, not exclusive groups, always being open and welcoming to new members. They need to attend to each other's needs, to take time for social events, retreats and other activities in order to build this bond. In my travels to parishes all over the country, I am shocked to encounter so many parish choirs that do not even know each other's names!

The choir needs to engage in outreach: to sing at nursing homes and hospitals, at schools and prisons, and to join in other activities that will build a sense of mission and not just satisfy their own musical fulfillment. When the choir invests in this kind of work (and it is work), the difference in their ministering on Sunday is astonishing. I am not talking about the naive, gooey, "we all love each other—isn't that wonderful" kind of dynamic, but the kind of musical leadership that models for the community a glimpse of what the reign of God should look like: a gathering of people committed to the Lord and one another who respond with the sharing of their gifts.

When communities are led by music ministers who have chosen to give that kind of commitment, it shows. The music making and the prayerful posture needed among our choirs takes care of itself. Choirs are called to be a "micro" church for the parish community. This new awareness should not be seen as something inferior to what the choir was called to before Vatican II, but just the opposite. Their role has been expanded to be a community of disciples serving God's people. It is a wonderful honor and privilege!

THE INSTRUMENTALISTS

Interestingly, in early Christian worship, instrumental music was often forbidden to take place in liturgical celebration. Our liturgical roots are grounded more in the ritual patterns of the Jewish home and synagogue than in those of the temple. There was always a strong sense that liturgical prayer was vocal—meaning sung—and that it reveled in the language and experience of singing and not in the disembodied sounds of instruments. Instrumental music in ancient Greece and Rome was associated with the activities of pagan cults and sacrifices, and thus inappropriate for sacred ritual worship. When polyphony developed in the repertoire, this attitude began to wane and various types of instruments began to be introduced into the liturgy.

Liturgical reform throughout history resulted in many different developments in instrumental music and the use of instruments in liturgy. This reached a culmination with the Second Vatican Council and *The Constitution on the Sacred Liturgy*, which excluded no instruments as long as they were in "accord with the dignity of the temple, and that they truly contribute to the edification of the faithful" (n. 120). Any classification and rating of instruments that claims to rank them according to their appropriateness within these criteria is snobbery driven by personal taste.

Many musicians and pastors have attempted to make their own personal preferences become policy, resulting in tyranny and confusion about what instruments are appropriate for use in worship. The issue here is not the instrument itself, but rather how the instrument is used in the liturgy. Official documentation sets the record clear:

> Musical instruments can be very useful in sacred celebrations, whether they accompany the singing or whether they are played as solo instruments. "The pipe organ is to be held in high esteem...." "The use of other instruments may also be admitted in divine worship...." In permitting and using musical instruments, the culture and traditions of individual peoples must be taken into account.... Any musical instrument permitted in divine worship should be used in a way that it meets the needs of the liturgical celebration, and is in the interests both of beauty of worship and the edification of the faithful.[5]

The repertoire being composed for music today offers many different instrumental combinations and approaches. In addition to the organ, the piano and the guitar have gained respect and remain in the mainstream of most parish liturgical settings. The repertoire and skill level of many musicians continues to improve and grow. Additional instruments—woodwinds, brass, synthesizers and percussion—also enhance many liturgical ensembles.

The rise of technology has affected the liturgical ensemble as well. Synthesizers have become more and more popular in their use and implementation, and, when competently used, can very effectively complete the ensemble. Some concerns have arisen with the new acceptance of technology, especially regarding the use of sequencers and prerecorded music. Parishes do exist where this technology is actually replacing competent musicians in leading parish music. This is a most dangerous development indeed. We should never attempt to replace the dynamic of human beings making music with machines and computers. Ritual, while possessing a structure, is still an organic, breathing and spontaneous event open to being acted upon by the effects of the environment in which it occurs, the gifts of those gathered and the work of the Spirit.

In any discussion of the role of the instrumentalist, we should remember that the singing voice of the assembly is the musical centerpiece of every liturgy. In other words, the role of the instrumentalist in the liturgy is to help enhance the common prayer of a singing assembly. The instruments we employ should never be the focus. We need to embrace a new "ministerial model" for parish liturgical instrumentalists (and all members of a liturgical music ensemble):

Parish instrumentalists and vocalists can only lead with integrity when they place the prayer of the community and the demands of the liturgy ahead of any particular instrument or style. For many instrumentalists, this requires a fundamental re-ordering of priorities in liturgy. This new orientation could be described as a "ministerial model." This ministerial model does not reject either the organ or the guitar, the traditional choir or the "folk" choir. In this model, however, the assembly's full participation in word and sacrament is the starting point for any consideration of how to lead music worship so that every element of the music making experience (instrumentation, repertoire, presentation style) is judged by how well it supports the prayer of all, how well it engages everyone present in a dialogical and prayerful celebration, and how well it points beyond itself to the praise of God.[6]

NOTES:

[1] *The Constitution on the Sacred Liturgy, Vatican Council II: The Conciliar and Post Conciliar Documents,* Austin Flannery, O.P., general editor (Northport, N.Y.: Costello Publishing Company, 1988), n. 114.

[2] *Music in Catholic Worship,* n. 21.

[3] Edward Foley, "The Cantor in Historical Perspective," in *Ritual Music: Studies in Liturgical Musicology* (Portland, Ore.: The Pastoral Press, 1995).

[4] *Liturgical Music Today,* Bishops' Committee on the Liturgy, United States Conference of Catholic Bishops, 1982, n. 68.

[5] "Instruction on Music in the Liturgy," *Constitution on the Sacred Liturgy,* nos. 62-63

[6] Marty Haugen. "The Third Way: A Ministerial Model for the Liturgical Ensemble," *Pastoral Music,* August-September 2000, pg. 38.

CHAPTER FIVE

*I*MAGES FOR THE MINISTER OF MUSIC

WHAT DOES IT TAKE to be a music minister? The following is a list of essential qualities, of defining characteristics for those who engage in the ministry of music. Some of these characteristics may be obvious, but some may be new to you; I hope all are helpful.

THE MUSIC MINISTER IS A MUSICIAN

Whoever speaks must do so as one speaking the very words of God.... —*(1 Peter 4:11)*

For music ministers, the sentence should be: "Whoever sings must do so as one singing the very words of God."

The minister of music should possess or work toward developing some basic talent, competence in reading music, singing or proficiency at their instrument, as well as overall musicianship. This is not meant to be an elitist pronouncement. If someone wants to be a minister of music and does not know how to read music, or is in some way deficient in musical skills, this does not mean they are not welcome. But we should all want to grow beyond our limitations. We should not be satisfied with our present level of skills, regardless of how much musical training we may or may not have. The music minister should always be concerned with enhancing their musical skills, always eager to improve and grow. We never "graduate" or grow out of the need to practice, rehearse and deepen our expertise musically.

We need to listen, learn and be open to all kinds of musical expressions. Music ministers should be musicians who are constantly listening, going to concerts and exploring different musical genres beyond their own personal tastes. It shocks me when someone says, for example, that they hate opera, and then follows that by saying they have never been to one!

We should listen to everything: classical, pop, jazz, country, rap, folk and indigenous music, Broadway, rhythm and blues, and other expressions in the galaxy of musical styles and genres. When we do so, we expand our sonic vocabulary and our understanding of what appeals to different kinds of people.

Whether or not we like a certain kind of music is not what is important, but if we are to be good musicians, it is our responsibility to be aware and to stretch ourselves to learn and grow from other musicians and from different perspectives and styles. We may come to learn and appreciate, and even enjoy, a kind of music that we would never have thought possible before. When we stretch outside our musical comfort zones, we can begin to honor how other people pray and celebrate. If this attitude were more evident, the "style wars" that pervade parish life would be fewer, and we could get on with the business of serving people in our life of communal prayer.

THE MUSIC MINISTER IS A PERFORMER AND ARTIST

It was the duty of the trumpeters and singers to make themselves heard in unison in praise and thanksgiving to the LORD, and when the song was raised, with trumpets and cymbals and other musical instruments, in praise to the LORD,
  "For he is good,
    for his steadfast love endures forever,"
the house, the house of the LORD, was filled with a cloud, so that the priests could not stand to minister because of the cloud; for the glory of the LORD filled the house of God.
—*2 Chronicles 5:13–14*

Isn't this a wonderful image of what liturgy should be? While we should be concerned that liturgical music not be a performance for performance's sake, we should be equally concerned with the quality of our music making. We should never be satisfied with our preparations and skills being "good enough." Music ministers must grow and understand quality performance (in the best sense of the word) and artistry in what they do, never being satisfied with mediocrity. Music ministers are artists who realize that the true work of art that they are creating is Jesus Christ, and they are always aware that prayer and worship is the canvas on which they paint.

The minister of music should be concerned with beauty, quality and excellence. Why should the music on Sunday be the worst we hear all week long?

THE MUSIC MINISTER LOVES COMMUNAL SINGING

…be filled with the Spirit, as you sing psalms and hymns and spiritual songs among yourselves, singing and making melody to the Lord in your hearts…. —*Ephesians 5:18b–19*

The minister of music must be intoxicated and seduced by the sound of a singing assembly. It has been said, "The pastoral musician must learn to love the sound of a singing congregation above any other sound."[1] Some of the best music ministers are musicians who know how to lead a sing-a-long. Everything we do, every choice we make and every decision and strategy has to have this participatory goal in mind, regardless of whether we are cantors, choir members or instrumentalists.

THE MUSIC MINISTER IS A LEADER, BUT ALSO A TEAM PLAYER

Speak, for your servant is listening. —*1 Samuel 3:10*

Then I heard the voice of the Lord saying, "Whom shall I send, and who will go for us?" And I said, "Here am I; send me!" —*Isaiah 6:8*

All who believed were together.... —*Acts 2:44a*

While our call is to serve, we as ministers should never apologize for our role or shy away from its responsibility. We need to lead, with strength and confidence, yet at the same time be attentive and compassionate. This is a difficult balance to achieve. For directors of choirs and ensembles, this kind of leadership is essential. Our praying congregations are starving for strong and bold leadership from all of our ministers. While humility is an important quality in leaders, our people also need passion and enthusiasm. Far too often humility leads to wimpy leadership. However, no prima donnas or divas are allowed. Father Ray East likes to say, "Diva out—Jesus in! Ego out—Jesus in!" The minister of music always works in partnership and tandem with other musicians and other ministers of the liturgy, never in isolation. Collaboration is key to effective ministry.

Collaborative leadership does not dismiss the need for leaders to make courageous and, at times, unpopular decisions. Decisions should be made not to make people happy, but rather, to serve the broader concerns of the parish and its common prayer together.

Leadership means not being trapped by our fear and addiction to being liked. A true leader is not always popular. There are two phrases that often become the undoing of leaders in parish life: "Our people are not ready for that yet," and "We've always done it that way." Bowing to these approaches will not result in leadership and growth, however prevalent and insidious they may be.

THE MUSIC MINISTER IS A PERSON OF HOSPITALITY

Whoever welcomes you welcomes me, and whoever welcomes me welcomes the one who sent me. —*Matthew 10:40*

What is a grandmother? A grandmother is a woman who had no children of her own. A grandfather is a man grandmother. He goes for walks with the boys, and they talk about fishing and stuff like that. Grandmothers don't have to do anything except "be there." They are so old, they should never play hard or run. They should slow down when they come by things like pretty leaves and caterpillars—they should never say: "hurry up." Grandmothers are usually fat, but not too fat to tie your shoes. They wear glasses and funny underwear, and they can even take their teeth and gums off. Everyone should try to have a grandmother, especially if you don't have a TV. Because they are the only ones among all of the grown-ups, who have time. *(A third-grade girl)*

This charming little essay holds great wisdom for us to understand the true ministry of hospitality. Hospitality is about making time, about making intentional efforts to reach out beyond ourselves. Hospitality is more than saying "hello" or "good morning." Hospitality says more profoundly, "when you are not here, we are less the body of Christ." Ministers (including music ministers) are people who go outside themselves, out of their way for the sake of another. In many of our parish liturgies, the cantor or other music minister is the first person to greet or be seen by the assembly. We are not hospitable to be nice. Like the disciples who welcomed Jesus on the road to Emmaus, we are hospitable to provide an encounter with the risen Lord. To be in service is to give of oneself, to be inconvenienced for another. This is what it means to serve.

A general policy to be encouraged in parishes is to make sure that all music ministers are prepared and ready at least fifteen minutes before the liturgy begins. This means the music is lined up, instruments are tuned, and all rehearsing and private prayer time is finished. In these minutes before the liturgy, instead of hiding in the sacristy or staying among themselves, all the members of the music ministry should spread out and fill the corners of the church and gathering space to welcome and greet those coming to celebrate. This is especially critical for cantors. This helps to develop relationships, and immediately enables more effective leadership and ministry to the people being led in prayer.

Music ministers should also not leave immediately after the closing song, but should stay behind and be available to the folks, should visit over coffee and doughnuts after the liturgy and continue nurturing relationships among the members of the parish. This is not icing on the cake, this is becoming and empowering human manifestations of the presence of Christ.

THE MUSIC MINISTER LOVES THE LITURGY

> They devoted themselves to the apostles' teaching and fellowship, to the breaking of bread and the prayers. —*Acts 2:42*

To be a responsible minister of sung prayer we must join ourselves closely to the prayer of the church and strive to learn about the elements of good worship and ritual. This requires ongoing learning, study and reflection. Opportunities for reading and study abound, and more liturgical music conferences and workshops are available than ever before. Music ministers should take advantage of these opportunities to deepen their understanding of worship, symbol, sacrament and ritual action.

THE MUSIC MINISTER IS A LOVER OF PEOPLE

> This is my commandment, that you love one another as I have loved you. No one has greater love than this, to lay down one's life for one's friends. —*John 15:12–13*

While this command to love one another may be obvious, it amazes me sometimes that many people involved in liturgical music do not like people very much. This is an appalling stance for anyone in ministry. Ministers of music should always embrace belonging to a group of people, the parish assembly. Christ is most profoundly present in the gift of human beings. We do not come from the outside, to do a Sunday gig, but rather, we are an invested member of our own Christian community.

THE MUSIC MINISTER IS *NOT* A MUSICAL OBSTRUCTIONIST

Do not speak evil against one another, brothers and sisters.… So who, then, are you to judge your neighbor?… do not grumble against one another, so that you may not be judged.
—*James 4:11, 12b; 5:9a*

Praise him with trumpet sound;
    praise him with lute and harp!
Praise him with tambourine and dance;
    praise him with strings and pipe!
Praise him with clanging cymbals;
    praise him with loud clashing cymbals!
Let everything that breathes praise the LORD. —*Psalm 150:3–6*

The battle of musical tastes and styles is still present in many liturgical circles and, unfortunately, in the everyday life of our praying communities. These prevailing attitudes of arrogance and judgment can poison worship. Ministers of music need to lead the way to disinfect our prayer of this tyranny of musical snobbery. If we are to call ourselves ministers of music, we must be musicians open to all styles, to the many expressions in which God is celebrated and known to us.

Contrary to popular belief, God does not prefer any one musical style over another. Psalm 150 proclaims that not only are all instruments allowed to be used in worship, but more adamantly, it mandates that everything that can possibly make a sound is compelled to praise and give worship to God. God *does,* however, care that we execute our ministry with integrity and a sense of prayerful leadership.

THE MUSIC MINISTER IS A PERSON OF PASTORAL CARE

Pursue love and strive for the spiritual gifts, and especially that you may prophesy. For those who speak in a tongue do not speak to other people but to God; for nobody understands them, since they are speaking mysteries in the Spirit. On the other hand, those who prophesy speak to other people for their upbuilding and encouragement and consolation. Those who speak in a tongue build up themselves, but those who prophesy build up the church. —*1 Corinthians 14:1–4*

The simplest way to say this is that people always come first. Our ministry should not serve our own personal musical palate or aesthetic sensibilities, but be grounded in the ordinary struggles, hurts and longings of the human spirit. If you are a minister of music, you are a servant of the community, a "wounded healer," with Jesus as the model. All prayer leadership exists for the common good of the community, and all good prayer leaders care about people and their needs, their dreams, their hopes, questions and fears.

THE MUSIC MINISTER IS A PERSON OF GRATITUDE

And be thankful. —*Colossians 3:15b*

Good ministry comes from some experience of gratitude and thankfulness. When we are grateful, we are not jealous of someone else. When we are thankful, we are not threatened when someone else gets the solo. When we feel grateful, we are not as concerned about whether or not our opinion is adopted. When we are filled with gratitude, we are no longer imprisoned by the prison of ourselves, and we can see the many blessings before us and around us in our fellow ministers, and in the assembly whom we serve.

We offer our gifts as ministers of music with humility, and we recognize it to be an honor and a privilege to do so. If we lose that, we lose authentic ministry. Meister Eckhart wrote, "If the only prayer I ever prayed was 'thank you,' that would be enough."

THE MUSIC MINISTER IS A PERSON CONCERNED WITH JUSTICE

I hate, I despise your...solemn assemblies.
    Even though you offer me your burnt offerings...
Take away from the noise of your songs;
    I will not listen to the melody of your harps.
But let justice roll down like waters,
    and righteousness like an everflowing stream. —*Amos 5:21–24*

Take all the lost home,
walk close by the children,
and comfort the old ones.[2]

To sing about God's reign and not be committed to justice in our community, in the church at large and in the world is to sing only lies. We need to remember what the prophet Amos has proclaimed to us.

It is easy and tempting to water down the message of justice making, or to think that it is not the role of the music minister to proclaim this challenge. Ministers of music need intentionally to reflect upon the texts they sing in this regard, and to examine their own efforts beyond their music making in reaching out beyond themselves. The various musical ensembles in the parish should make commitments for experiences in which they leave the cocoon of the worship space. We need to visit the soup kitchens, the prisons and the hospitals and get our hands dirty doing the work and action that we regularly sing about on Sunday. These conversion moments become powerful when music ministers have the commitment and courage to do more than sing the notes and words.

To be doers of justice is not optional for Christians. It is a mandate, initiated in us at the moment of our baptism. Music ministers are not only asked to share in this mandate, they are called to help lead the way.

THE MUSIC MINISTER IS A PERSON ALWAYS ON THE PATH OF ONGOING SPIRITUAL GROWTH

And now bless the God of all,
> who everywhere works great wonders,
> who fosters our growth from birth…—*Sirach 50:22*

I planted, Apollos watered, but God gave the growth. —*1 Corinthians 3:6*

Burnout and cynicism may seep into our lives unless we take care of ourselves spiritually and find spiritual companions with whom to share our life of faith. Whether we read and pray alone with Scripture, or find a group to pray with, or make an annual retreat, or regularly consult a spiritual director or mentor—whatever the approach—we need to have a concrete and disciplined path that will keep us grounded with our God, both personally and in relationship with others.

THE MUSIC MINISTER IS A PERSON OF PASSION

Blessed be the God and Father of our Lord Jesus Christ, who has blessed us in Christ with every spiritual blessing in the heavenly places, just as he chose us in Christ before the foundation of the world to be holy and blameless before him in love. He destined us for adoption as his children through Jesus Christ, according to the good pleasure of his will, to the praise of his glorious grace that he freely bestowed on us in the Beloved…. In Christ we have also obtained an inheritance, having been destined according to the purpose of him who accomplishes all things according to his counsel and will, so that we, who were the first to set our hope on Christ, might live for the praise of his glory. In him you also, when you had heard the word of truth, the gospel of your sal-

vation, and had believed in him, were marked with the seal of the promised Holy Spirit; this is the pledge of our inheritance toward redemption as God's own people, to the praise of his glory.
—*Ephesians 1:3–6, 11–14*

Ministers of music must be deeply committed and passionate about their ministry, about their parish, about people, about the liturgy, about their faith and about Jesus, who is at the center of all things, and at the center of all ministry. Ministers of music in a most unique, creative and powerful way, proclaim the Christian life. If we are not struggling to be living embodiments of fidelity and passion for the gospel, then we have no business standing in front of a praying assembly—we profane our ministry.

We proclaim hope, a hope for which our communities are thirsting, they are deserving of nothing less than one hundred percent from us in our efforts.

These images challenge all of us as music ministers to embrace the vocation of liturgical music as a true call, and not to serve merely as musical "helpers." The church challenges us as well:

What motivates the pastoral musician? Why does he or she give so much time and effort to the service of the church at prayer? The only answer can be that the church musician is first a disciple and then a minister. The musician belongs first of all to the assembly; he or she is a worshiper above all. Like any member of the assembly, the pastoral musician needs to be a believer, needs to experience conversion, needs to hear the Gospel and so proclaim the praise of God. Thus, the pastoral musician is not merely an employee or volunteer. He or she is a minister, someone who shares faith, serves the community and expresses the love of God and neighbor through music.[3]

NOTES

[1] Charlie Gardner, "Ten Commandments for Liturgical Musicians," *Pastoral Music,* April/May 1983, p. 38.

[2] Joe Wise, "Take All the Lost Home," copyright ©1977, Fontaine House/GIA Publications, Chicago. All rights reserved.

[3] *Liturgical Music Today,* n. 64.

CHAPTER SIX

*W*HAT KIND OF MUSIC DO WE NEED?

TO UNDERSTAND FULLY the nature of good liturgical music, and to implement competently sound musical choices, we have to discover and reflect upon the musical and ritual forms that blossom from our liturgical structures. It is helpful to begin by understanding what separates *liturgical* music from other kinds of religious music. In their 1972 document *Music in Catholic Worship,* the Bishops' Committee on the Liturgy expanded upon three "judgements" that, they said, must be made to determine the value of a given musical element in a liturgical celebration. A brief examination of each of these three criteria follows.

THE MUSICAL JUDGMENT

This judgment pertains to musical quality. The document poses this question, "Is the music technically, aesthetically, and expressively good?" (*MCW* # 26). However, what makes music *good* can be subjective. The document begins to clarify its position: "To admit the cheap, the trite, the musical cliché…is to cheapen the liturgy, to expose it to ridicule, and invite failure" (*MCW* # 26). But a careful distinction is made between *quality* and *style*.

> We do a disservice to musical values, however, when we confuse the judgment of music with the judgment of musical style. Style and value are two distinct judgments. Good music of new styles is finding a happy home in the celebrations of today…. We must judge value within each style.[1]

So, style and genre aside, what makes for good music in the liturgical context? The answer can be found in describing what makes for good music in any situation: a sense of form, rhythmic vitality and a good melodic contour. Good compositional craft is fundamental, regardless of whether the piece of music is a hymn, a chorale, folk style or pop/rock inspired. The tools and elements that make for good music do not go away because of musical style or the competence of the musical leaders.

THE LITURGICAL JUDGMENT

Employing liturgical judgment, we ask: Does the music help support the liturgical action? This type of judgment distinguishes between liturgical music and sacred or inspirational music. While these other kinds of religious music may meet musical judgment considerations and have a good message, they may not necessarily form a good partnership with the liturgical actions and ritual units found in liturgical celebration.

First among concerns of liturgical judgment is whether or not the music is participatory. If the music is centered on a soloist or small group of performers, it may be inspiring, but it does not engage a congregation in communal prayer. While the music may be beautiful and embody a sacred text (for example, the "Hallelujah Chorus," or César Franck's *Panis Angelicus),* it is not music that can intensify and bring to life a communal ritual moment. Some fundamental questions to ask include: Who sings the music? At what time? Do the liturgical moments wedded to song respect the primacy of the assembly in their participation? Are the roles of cantor, choir and instrumentalist in sync with these concerns?

The structure of the rite is also a most important consideration. When planning and making choices, it is the liturgy itself that determines what music is needed and called for. The importance and priority of the liturgical moment should be matched by the piece of music that is wedded to it. If the assembly sings a rousing hymn at the Preparation of the Gifts, complete with brass and SATB choir, followed by a whimpering unison "Holy, Holy" during the Eucharistic Prayer, the result will be disproportionate. This is one of many reasons ministers of music need to study the qualities of good liturgy and ritual.

Finally, the quality of the music itself cannot override the equal and often more important consideration of the text. Does the music help express the text? Is the text inclusive? Does the text echo the Word proclaimed and preached at this celebration? Do the metaphors build the communal nature of worship? Is it good poetry, rich in symbolic and metaphoric language? Does this text proclaim good theology, steeped in Scripture and other sources of the tradition?

THE PASTORAL JUDGMENT

Pastoral judgment is the most difficult and elusive judgment of all, yet at the same time it is the most important. The purpose of music in the liturgy is not to satisfy our musical sensibilities or to make the liturgy an end in itself. Liturgy is communal prayer designed to deepen faith and call believers to mission, and the role of music is to help free a gathered assembly to enter into that prayer. Thus it is from the pastoral judgment that the challenging question arises: "Does music in this celebration enable these people to express their faith, in this place, in this age, in this culture?" (*MCW* # 39). This concern needs to be at the center of the entire liturgical enterprise, in the stages of preparation, celebration and in our evaluation of our parish liturgical life. If we, as liturgical and musical leaders, refuse to consider the pastoral judgment, we are then merely making music and acting out rituals for our own amusement and satisfaction:

> A musician may judge that a certain composition or style of composition is good music, but this musical judgment really says nothing about whether and how this music is to be used in this cel-

ebration. The signs of the celebration must be accepted and received as meaningful for a genuinely human faith experience for these specific worshippers. This pastoral judgment can be aided by sensitivity to the cultural and social characteristics of the people who make up the congregation: their age, culture, and education. These factors influence the effectiveness of the liturgical signs, including music. No set of rubrics or regulations of itself will ever achieve a truly pastoral celebration of the sacramental rites. Such regulations must always be applied with a pastoral concern for the given worshipping community.[2]

Now that we have examined these three types of judgment and how they relate to each other, we can turn to an examination of the musical and liturgical forms that are part of our liturgical tradition. These forms help actualize communal worship.

MUSICAL AND LITURGICAL FORMS

LET THERE BE ACCLAMATIONS...

An acclamation is a communal shout, a ritual expression that shapes our belief system. In the simplest terms, an acclamation is an investment, not just mere assent. Good strong acclamations are critical to liturgical worship, have primacy over other repertoire considerations and should be at the center of concern in musical and liturgical planning. Acclamations become the voice for the assembly in expressing their rightful role as first-class participants in worship. Acclamations are short and rhythmically and musically strong. They are almost always repetitive and, at their best, sung by heart:

> The acclamations are shouts of joy which arise from the whole assembly as forceful and meaningful assents to God's Word and Action. They are important because they make some of the most significant moments of the Mass…stand out. It is of their nature that they be rhythmically strong, melodically appealing, and affirmative. The people should know the acclamations by heart in order to sing them spontaneously.[3]

The acclamatory texts in the context of the Eucharist are primarily the Gospel acclamation and the acclamations during the Eucharistic Prayer (the Holy, the Memorial Acclamation and the Great Amen). Other acclamations in liturgical celebrations include the blessing and sprinkling of the assembly with water and the many acclamations called for in the many initiation liturgies. These include acclamations that accompany the signing of the senses at the Rite of Acceptance, and acclamations that accompany the actual baptisms and renewal of baptismal promises at the Easter Vigil.

Acclamations are at the heart and center of our worship structure, giving the weight necessary for the primary liturgical actions and moments; they help empower and form the assembly as co-celebrants in the liturgy.

LET THERE BE LITANIES AND DIALOGIC MUSIC...

Litanies and musical dialogues express the very essence of ritual language—the "proclamation-response" pattern that is a common thread in any liturgical celebration. The liturgy begins every Sunday with the presider proclaiming, "The Lord be with you," and we respond automatically by heart, "and also with you." This form of "proclamation-response" is ritually how we express God's relationship with us. God initiates activity with us, and we respond in faith.

Litanies and dialogues are most recognized in the Penitential Rite, the General Intercessions and the Lamb of God/Fraction Rite. In a good litany the movement and progression of the dialogue moves beyond the specific intonations and results in a communal act of worship and awe. This requires that the length of the litany be substantial, as two or three invocations will not accomplish this. The specific text of the litany is not as important as is the repetition of the response, which in and of itself becomes a prayer of intercession.

Other litanies that are part of our worship repertoire are the Litany of the Saints, or songs that use a call-and-response pattern, such as the well-known gospel song, "O Healing River."

LET THERE BE MANTRAS AND OSTINATOS...

While having origins in Eastern cultures and meditation practices, the mantra has become a wonderful liturgical form. Part of our Catholic devotional life (the prayer of the rosary, for example), the mantra has found increased value as a musical genre, most recently made known and available to us in many of the creative musical settings that have risen out of the Taizé community in France. Like the litany, the goal of using the mantra is to become completely lost in the repetitive act, to let the music and prayer take the worshippers into a place of contemplation and presence.

Mantra settings would work well for many places in the liturgy, as a call to worship or Gathering Song, as Responsorial Psalm, in the General Intercessions or as a communal processional, to name just a few. Outside of eucharistic celebrations, mantras can also be effective during communal ritual actions of reconciliation, anointing of the sick and devotional or adoration experiences.

LET THERE BE PSALMODY...

The early songs of Israel were also the prayers of Jesus and are at the heart of prayer in any liturgical setting. Psalms are lyrical in nature and should always be sung. They represent and express the deepest emotions of human experience: joy, praise, hope, despair, anger, rage, contentment and the feelings associated with pilgrimage:

> What is more important than a psalm? David himself puts it nicely: "Praise the Lord," he says, "for a psalm is good" (Psalm 146:1). And indeed! A psalm is the blessing of the people, the praise of God, the commendation of the multitude, the applause of all, the speech of every person, the voice of the church, the sonorous profession of faith, devotion full of authority, the joy of liberty, the noise of good cheer, and the echo of gladness. It softens anger, it gives release from anxiety,

it alleviates sorrow; it is protection at night, instruction by day, a shield in time of fear, a feast of holiness, the image of tranquility, a pledge of peace and harmony, which produces one song from various and sundry voices in the manner of a cithara. The day's dawning resounds with a psalm, with a psalm its passing echoes.[4]

In addition to the importance of the Responsorial Psalm during the Liturgy of the Word, psalms may be considered for other liturgical moments as well—gathering and recessional processions, communion songs and so on. The psalms also are at the center of communal celebrations of the Liturgy of the Hours, most notably morning and evening prayer.

The usual approach to psalm singing in liturgical worship in recent years has been the refrain-verse style, with the assembly having a common refrain with the cantor or choir singing the verses. Certain psalms, however, have a different internal structure, such as Psalm 136, where the structure of the text calls for a litanic response integrated in its presentation. There are also many wonderful translations of the psalms in strophic form and using an ostinato refrain with accompanying verses. All of these structures reflect the depth of the Psalter. We, as music ministers, need to explore more deeply these ritual structures, become more biblically literate in the content of the psalms and choose quality settings for the liturgy, especially for the Responsorial Psalm.

LET THERE BE SONGS...

The explosion of liturgical music reform in recent years is evident in the use of song form (refrain and verse) in very successful ways. The most obvious and necessary element of the celebration of Eucharist that calls for song is the table song, sung during the sharing of the bread and cup. Other ritual moments where song can be used include during the Preparation of the Gifts, as a song of thanksgiving after the sharing of Communion or during the gathering song, sprinkling or dismissal.

LET THERE BE HYMNODY...

While acclamations, litanies and psalmody are at the center of liturgical song, hymns still hold an important place in Roman Catholic worship. While secondary in importance to the place of acclamations, litanies and psalmody, hymns still provide an important prayer form.

Part of the problem we have had with hymns lies in how we have utilized them in our pastoral practice. It is unfortunate that Catholics over the years have not experienced hymns the way many Protestant traditions have. For other Christian traditions, hymns are actual sources of their theology. Many seminaries in non-Roman Catholic traditions require classes in hymnody and hymn texts for ordination candidates. Hymns can be rich sources for preaching and theological reflection. Protestants have strong memories of the family gatherings around the piano in their homes for hymn singing. For many Catholics, hymns are experienced as "traveling music" or "filler." Most appallingly, Catholics rarely sing all of the stanzas of a hymn. We have chosen to implement their use at some of the most unimportant places in the liturgical celebration; we use hymns to accompany the priest moving to and from the sanctuary and to take up the collection. We need to recover a rich and treasured use of hymns in worship.

First, we need to stop chopping up the stanzas, and understand that a good hymn text (like any other literary form) has a clear beginning, content and conclusion. Quality hymns are complete and full prayer structures, and this is destroyed both by the omission of stanzas and by the dreadful presentation that they have often been given.

Hymns can also echo well the story of our tradition. They take us back as we sing them as the songs of our ancestors and help us to remember where we came from. A vast richness of hymnody is available to us from other traditions in addition to the storehouse of our Roman Catholic treasury. We have not even begun to tap the resources that exist in hymnody. Good, strong and vigorous hymn singing is a powerful spiritual action.

A primary moment for the hymn in the liturgy is at the song of gathering, which the assembly should sing in its entirety. Hymns can also be utilized as a response to the homily, borrowing from our Protestant brothers and sisters, who have a tradition of the "hymn of the day," following strongly in line with the Scriptures of the day. Hymns also work well as songs of thanksgiving after the sharing of communion, or as music to dismiss the assembly.

LET THERE BE CHANT AND CANTILLATION...

With the ongoing explosion of new forms, we often forget or dismiss the rich storehouse of chant which offers access to the collective memory of our tradition and our expressions of worship and faith.

A perceived difficulty with chant is that it is hard to put it in concert with the principles of participatory singing, because much of the chant may seem too difficult and complex melodically for the average congregation to sing.

However, it is hard to imagine Advent without singing "O Come, O Come Emmanuel," or "Creator Alde Siderum," or to celebrate Holy Thursday without "Pange Lingua." As with our presentation of hymnody, the problem often lies with our inadequate and, at times, dirge-like approach in leading and singing chant. Quality chant and cantillation is heightened ritual speech, very much at the heart of many of our most treasured ritual moments: the water blessings, the Exsultet at the Easter Vigil, the blessing of oil at a communal anointing, the ritual moments of the Kyrie, Agnus Dei and free intercessory prayer.

We need not ignore our wonderful chant repertoire, but open ourselves again to its richness, re-present it and adapt it for our present, post-Vatican II worship environment.

LET THERE BE RITUAL MUSIC FOR THE SACRAMENTS AND OTHER LITURGICAL CELEBRATIONS...

In addition to providing good, sound and prayerful music for our primary Sunday celebrations and liturgical feasts, music ministers are called to help enliven the many other liturgical and sacramental celebrations through the creative implementation of ritual music.

Good acclamations, litanies, processional songs, psalms and mantras are needed for the various rites of Christian initiation, both for the adult rites and communal celebrations of infant baptism and confirmation. We need good ritual music for communal reconciliation, acclamatory responses to the examination of conscience and songs of praise leading up to the ritual actions of absolution.

Weddings always provide many pastoral challenges to help the assembly be participants, not observers. We need acclamations from the assembly to affirm the consent of the couple, and musical settings of the nuptial blessing that engage the assembly in their role as witnesses and companions for the journey. For communal services of anointing, we need good music to accompany the blessing of the oil, and to accompany the gestures of laying on of hands and anointing.

Funerals, of course, hold powerful moments in which music can truly touch, heal and give solace and comfort to those experiencing grief. Music can intensify the moments of the placing of the pall, cross and Word on the casket; song provides solidarity during the moments of final commendation and prayers at the graveside. Good music implemented in the celebrations of ministry, such as ordinations, professions and commissioning services, offers opportunity for the assembly to be challenged to share the ministry of those who are making these intense and intentional commitments.

Many other celebrations call musicians to muster their gifts and creativity, such as celebrations of the Liturgy of the Hours (especially morning and evening prayer) that are becoming more popular and experiencing a rebirth in parish life. School liturgies, catechetical celebrations and prayer services for young people of all ages, especially celebrations of Liturgy of the Word for children, are also events that demand great care and attention from ministers of music. Music for numerous other liturgical celebrations, such as the dedication of a church, benediction, blessings and Marian celebrations, can help draw people into the communal action.

No liturgical event or prayer service should take place without song. Regardless of the specific liturgical celebration, focus or event, the same grounding principles come into play for those entrusted in leading music.

LET THERE BE MUSIC OF MANY STYLES AND CULTURES...

We need to recognize the value and honor the variety of expressions in the vast landscape of the entire people of God. We are a people who come from history, proclaiming a story that had and has its own voice. These various expressions need to be reverenced and held high.

We also have to remember where we are now and where we are going. While prophetic liturgy is always counter-cultural in its message, it must also reflect who and where we are in time and place. Only then can we be transformed to travel to an unknown country. Elitism in musical style must not be tolerated, regardless of one's musical bias:

> We do a disservice to musical values, however, when we confuse the judgment of music with the judgment of musical style. Style and value are two distinct judgments.... We must judge value within each style.[5]

In other words, there is good music and poor music. There are good quality hymns, and there are poorly crafted hymns. There are good contemporary liturgical songs, and songs that are weak. The rules and criteria for good music (and good liturgical music), remain constant in musical craftsmanship: good melodic structure, strong rhythmic base, well thought out form. These qualities exist regardless of the particular style or genre utilized.

The wars between different musical camps still linger in our parishes, and we should heighten our resolve to end this destructive environment. Our lack of tolerance for this musical snobbery must be strengthened. Our God is greater than a single musical taste. God can be and is made known and celebrated in the beauty of polyphony and chant. The Good News is celebrated in popular melodic song and in the rousing energy of southern gospel or the spiritual. The presence of the holy is found in the honest strains of traditional folk melodies and instruments and in the grandeur of the finest pipe organ and antiphonal brass. We hear God's revelation in the innocence of a children's choir as well as in the sturdiness of the chorale and the traditional hymn. The diversity of our music reflects the diversity of our communities:

> Can the same parish liturgy be an authentic expression for a grade school girl, her college-age brother, their married sister with her young family, their parents and grandparents? Can it satisfy the theologically and musically educated along with those lacking in training? Can it please those who seek a more informal style of celebration? The planning team must consider the general makeup of the total community. Each Christian must keep in mind that to live and worship in community often demands a personal sacrifice. All must be willing to share likes and dislikes with those whose ideas and experience may be quite unlike their own.[6]

It is also important to reflect on the European-American bias found in our worship styles and in our music. Without casting out this influence in which there is much to reverence and treasure, we have to remember that we are not a church of a single culture, but a global village made up of many languages, cultural patterns and diverse spiritualities. In North America alone, we are a church that reflects the mosaic of our history. This diversity has important implications for the church. The same is the case for the way we worship and for the songs we sing. We have to remember that we belong to each other, and only by sharing each others' stories, intersecting and connecting with another horizon and tradition can we image the entire tapestry of the many faces of Christ:

> Even in linguistically and ethnically homogenous communities, singing the music of another culture means entering into their world. While by no means a complete introduction, the musical symbol can serve as a bridge into another culture.... Learning to sing another culture's music is not only a musical venture but also a way to enter their image of church, of salvation and of the paschal mystery itself.[7]

NOTES

[1] *Music in Catholic Worship*, n. 28.

[2] *Music in Catholic Worship*, n. 41.

[3] *Music in Catholic Worship*, n. 53.

[4] Saint Ambrose, in *Music in Early Christian Literature*, James McKinnon, editor (New York: Cambridge University Press, 1987), quoted in *A Sourcebook about Liturgy* (Chicago: Liturgy Training Publications, 1994), pp. 32-33.

[5] *Music in Catholic Worship*, n. 28.

[6] *Music in Catholic Worship*, n. 17.

[7] *The Milwaukee Symposia for Church Composers: A Ten Year Report*, n. 63.

CHAPTER SEVEN

THE LITURGY AND ITS ELEMENTS

WITH A CLEAR UNDERSTANDING of liturgical principles and the role of music in ritual, we have a foundation for the vision and elements of good liturgical celebration. The Vatican II renewal of the liturgy has provided an order, a structure for our normative Sunday gathering, which we call the Mass, or the Eucharist. The chart that follows illustrates the sequence of the ritual structures and actions that make up the Roman Catholic liturgy, along with the ministerial intent of these elements.

STRUCTURE OF THE RITE[1]	SPIRITUALITY OF THE RITE
GATHERING	*MANY BECOMING ONE*
Hospitality	*Forming the community*
Preparation of the Assembly	*Opening statement of faith*
Song of Gathering*	
Greeting	
Sprinkling Rite**	
Penitential Rite*	*Praising God for mercy*
Glory to God**	
Opening Prayer	*The community focuses*
WORD	*TELLING THE STORIES*
Hebrew Scripture Reading	*Telling the ancestral story*
Responsorial Psalm*	*Icons for the total Word*
Christian Scripture Reading	*Telling more of the story*
Gospel Acclamation*	*Praising the Word alive*
Gospel Proclamation	*Telling the Good News*
Homily	*Preaching the Good News*
Special Rites (occasionally)	
Profession of Faith	*Stating our beliefs*
General Intercessions*	*Praying for the world*

TABLE	ACTING, THANKING AND SHARING IN MEMORY OF CHRIST
Preparation of the Table and Gifts*	*Preparing gifts (us, money, bread and wine)*
Prayer over the Gifts	
Eucharistic Prayer	*Blessing, praising, giving thanks*
Preface	
First Eucharistic Acclamation: Holy, Holy**	
Epiclesis	
Narrative of the Institution	
Second Eucharistic Acclamation: Memorial Acclamation**	
Intercessory Prayer	
Third Eucharistic Acclamation: Doxology/Amen**	
The Communion Rite	*Sharing the meal*
The Lord's Prayer*	*Praying as Jesus taught*
The Sign of Peace	*Extending community*
The Breaking of the Bread: Lamb of God**	*Breaking and pouring*
The Communion Sharing: Table Song**	*Becoming the Body of Christ*
Hymn/Song of Thanksgiving*	*Thanking God for gifts*
Prayer after Communion	*Summing it up*

GOING FORTH	BEING THE BODY OF LIFE
Announcements	*Being church*
Final Blessing*	*Going forth to love and serve*
Song of Mission*	

*can be sung   ** is always sung

While the liturgy should not be picked apart moment by moment and needs to be experienced as a whole, it can be helpful to take a deeper look at the musical moments found in the primary liturgical units (Gathering, Word, Table and Going Forth). Rather than delving into all of the liturgical elements, this examination will limit itself to a brief description of the musical elements and options that are the responsibility of the musical leadership.

GATHERING

The Gathering or Introductory Rites have developed and been adapted throughout our liturgical history, but the basic purpose and intent has not changed. The principle is clearly stated in our liturgical documentation:

> The purpose of these rites is to help the assembled people become a worshipping assembly and to prepare them for listening to God's Word and celebrating the Eucharist.[2]

The primary focus, therefore, is not on processions or the priest or other liturgical leaders, but, rather, on the gathered community. When choosing music or adapting any aspect of the liturgical structure, we must always keep the primacy of the assembly at the center of all consideration. The beginning of any celebration (liturgical or otherwise) is a most critical element.

PRELUDE / PREPARATION

The use of music before the actual liturgy begins, such as an instrumental prelude, or a solo or choral selection, can either enhance or deter the overall intent of the time of Gathering. Any music or approach that would seek to or result in the gathered assembly taking on a passive or listening role, should be avoided at all cost. If prelude music is implemented, the nature or mood of the selection needs to be given careful consideration.

Regardless of whether or not prelude music is taking place, having the cantor or music leader conduct a musical rehearsal with the assembly is strongly recommended. The purpose is more than just to teach a new piece of music. Such a rehearsal is, rather, an opportunity for the assembly to warm up and focus their attention on their role as an active, participatory community. It also sends a clear message from the ministers of music that they and the assembly are in partnership together, that the assembly has the invitation and responsibility to minister in relationship to each other in song, and in other participatory aspects of the liturgy.

SONG OF GATHERING

Our official documentation states clearly the purpose and intent of the opening song:

> The entrance song should create an atmosphere of celebration. It helps put the assembly in the proper frame of mind for listening to the Word of God. It helps people to become conscious of themselves as a worshipping community. The choice of texts for the entrance song should not conflict with these purposes.[3]

> The entrance song serves to gather and unite the assembly and set the tone for the celebration.[4]

Even though pastoral experience may prove otherwise, the focus or role of the opening song is not to accompany the procession of the priest or other ministers. The purpose of the opening song is for the community to articulate and offer its worship, and to help them focus for the liturgical celebration. The Song of Gathering is the opening "faith statement" of the gathered assembly; it serves to galvanize the room of individuals into a connected community of faith and prayer.

It is interesting to note that the liturgical rubrics do not require a procession of the priest and other ministers. Rather, the ministers are simply instructed to take their places. Sometimes the liturgical choreography of a grand procession down the middle aisle contributes to the misunderstanding of the true purpose of the song. If there is a choice to implement a procession or not, the music chosen should be assembly based, and a strophic, through-composed hymn is probably best, or a song of which the assembly can sing both the refrain and all the verses. Also, regardless of the form of the song chosen, the music should be sung in its entirety to help the assembly truly focus themselves for the celebration. In other words, the opening song is truly the opening prayer for all who have gathered.

RITE OF BLESSING AND SPRINKLING WITH HOLY WATER

Immediately after the Song of Gathering, and the Sign of the Cross and greeting, the Order of Mass offers several optional rites, the first being the rite of sprinkling. Used less often (unfortunately) than the penitential rite, this rite is an expression of our baptismal call, a ritual recommitment of our baptismal promises and identity. The use of the sprinkling rite is especially effective during the Easter season when baptisms are part of the liturgical celebration. The blessing of the water that occurs just before the assembly is sprinkled can creatively be a dialogue between the priest and the community when music in litany form is used. Music should accompany the actual sprinkling of the people. Many pieces of music could be used, and the Gloria can even be considered for use here. If possible, the best choice of music would be one that would allow the assembly to sing without any printed music and text in front of them so that the full visual intent of the symbol of water can be experienced.

PENITENTIAL RITE/KYRIE

The penitential rite is arguably one of the most misunderstood elements in the entire eucharistic liturgy. It is not intended to be a laundry list of our sins, nor is it meant to be an examination of conscience. Rather, it is a recalling of the awesome mercy of our God, and a pleading to God to continue to shower us with unconditional love and forgiveness. This is an optional rite and is used in place of the rite of sprinkling, but not in addition to it. The sacramentary offers us many adaptations and forms, all of which can be presented musically. The rite should be experienced as an acclamation of praise, rather than a dreary, penitential exercise in self-humiliation. The original Greek *Kyrie eleison* is translated as "a chant of praise," honoring Christ as the one who truly reigns over the darkness and pathology of sin. Christ is the victor over all that is ungodly and shows the lack of our desire to follow and be children of God.

Musically, the third option found in the sacramentary works best. The litanic nature of the form allows for a musical dialogue among the presider, the cantor and the assembly. Many musical settings for this option are available. Another suggestion is to consider using this form of the penitential rite as the actual Song of Gathering, especially during the season of Lent.

In any case, if the Penitential Rite is to be sung, it should be done with a clear purpose and intent in mind, and with the certainty that the musical setting helps communicate the true nature of this rite.

GLORIA

This early Christian hymn is inspired by the song sung at the birth of Jesus, originating from liturgical traditions in the East. When it entered Western liturgy, it was originally sung at Christmas, and later it began to be sung at celebrations where the bishop was the presiding celebrant. Introduction into the normative Sunday liturgy, except during the seasons of Advent and Lent, came during the eleventh and twelfth centuries. The Gloria is an exuberant proclamation of praise and when utilized it should *always* be sung. It should never be a solo selection by the choir—it is an assembly-based song.

Because of metrical problems presented in singing the entire text, many composers have created musical settings employing a refrain for the assembly with cantor or choir on the verses. In some of these settings, after the beginning of the piece, the assembly picks up the verses as well, which is wonderful. In my opinion, the Gloria should not be used every Sunday. Its special praise character should be reserved for use during the festive times of the liturgical year: Christmas Eve and the entire Christmas season, the Easter Vigil and the remaining Sundays leading up to and including Pentecost, and other festive celebrations, such as Holy Thursday, the Body and Blood of Christ (Corpus Christi), Trinity Sunday and Christ the King.

It is best when the Gloria is very familiar to the community, so that it may be sung by heart, eventually. Music ministers should limit the number of settings used by a community. The Gloria can also be used in other places in the liturgy, such as the Song of Gathering, or as song of praise after the sharing of Communion.

WORD

The Liturgy of the Word and the Liturgy of the Table (Eucharist) constitute the two primal aspects of the liturgical celebration and are equally important. Both celebrate the "presence of Christ" in passionate, intense and authentic ways. For the average Catholic, the Bible is still new and uncharted territory. Before Vatican II, we did not place much importance on reading and sharing Scripture. In the renewed liturgy, we have come to understand the Word as being an important focus, not only in the celebration of the Mass but in our entire life of faith as well. A catechetical effort is needed to form our communities into understanding that the reading and preaching of the Scriptures is not a prelude to the liturgy of the Eucharist, but an equal celebration of the presence of Christ. We are fed at the table of the ambo (also called the pulpit, where the Scriptures are proclaimed) in the same way that we feast from the table.

For those entrusted with liturgical planning, the readings of the Word for a particular celebration provide the focus and direction for homily content and for musical choices. Therefore, it is important that ministers of music pray over the Scriptures for each celebration, and become more and more knowledgeable of the content and themes that lie within. It is recommended that music leaders and liturgical planners read commentaries and have at their disposal other resources that can break open the deeper message of the Scriptures for a particular celebration. The readings provide the path for the entire liturgy and all of its individual aspects: the music, the homily and the environment.

For the minister of music, the musical elements that need our attention are the Responsorial Psalm, the Gospel Acclamation and the General Intercessions.

RESPONSORIAL PSALM

The Responsorial Psalm as part of the Liturgy of the Word has prominence in the musical choices that are to be made for any specific liturgical celebration, and for an entire season as well. We need to affirm the Responsorial Psalm as actually being the second reading—remember, the Responsorial Psalm is Scripture proclamation. While there is no lack of psalm settings, we must choose carefully. The selection needs to be represented well musically, using a sound translation or paraphrase, and be grounded in the emotional contour of the text.

The singing of the Responsorial Psalm comes from the ancient practice of the Jewish synagogue. This text used to be referred to as the "gradual," meaning "from the steps of the altar." While the familiar "refrain-verse" format is normative now, there are musical settings that can be rendered in either a strophic or metrical form.

When choosing music for the Responsorial Psalm, please remember that it should actually be a psalm. The lectionary offers a proper psalm for each Sunday and/or celebration, but a seasonal or "common" psalm can be used throughout a season as well. These common/seasonal psalms are as follows:

ADVENT:
Psalm 25: "To you, O Lord, I lift my soul."
Psalm 85: "Lord, show us your mercy and love."

CHRISTMAS:
Psalm 98: "All the ends of the earth have seen the saving power of God."

EPIPHANY:
Psalm 72: "Lord, every nation on earth will adore you."

LENT:
Psalm 51: "Be merciful, O Lord for we have sinned."
Psalm 91: "Be with me, Lord, when I am in trouble."
Psalm 130: "With the Lord there is mercy, and fullness of redemption."

HOLY WEEK:
Psalm 22: "My God, my God, why have you abandoned me?"

EASTER VIGIL:
Psalm 136: "God's love is everlasting."

EASTER:
Psalm 66: "Let all the earth cry out to God with joy, alleluia."
Psalm 118: "This is the day the Lord has made; let us rejoice and be glad."

ASCENSION:
Psalm 47: "God mounts his throne to shouts of joy."

PENTECOST:
Psalm 104: "Lord, send out your Spirit, and renew the face of the earth."

ORDINARY TIME:
Psalm 19: "Lord, you have the words of everlasting life."
Psalm 27: "The Lord is my light and my salvation."
Psalm 34: "Taste and see the goodness of the Lord."
Psalm 63: "My soul is thirsting for you, O Lord my God."
Psalm 95: "If today you hear his voice, harden not your hearts."
Psalm 100: "We are his people, the sheep of his flock."
Psalm 103: "The Lord is kind and merciful."
Psalm 122: "Let us go rejoicing to the house of the Lord."

However, a common seasonal psalm for all four Sundays of Advent, for example, should be used only as a transitional and teaching tool, to move the community toward singing and praying the more complete liturgical Psalter.

GOSPEL ACCLAMATION

The Gospel Acclamation, alongside the Gospel Proclamation and homily, makes up the climactic moment in the Liturgy of the Word. With its roots in the Old Testament, "Alleluia" means "praise the Lord." This acclamatory text is at the heart of both Jewish and Christian worship. Different in nature and intent from the Responsorial Psalm, the Gospel Acclamation serves to acclaim and announce the Gospel Proclamation that follows, proclaiming the presence of Christ in the Word. Its role is anticipatory:

> The Alleluia, or as the liturgical season requires, the verse before the gospel, is also a "rite or act standing by itself." It serves as the greeting of welcome of the assembled faithful to the Lord who is about to speak to them and as an expression of their faith through song. The Alleluia or the verse

before the gospel must be sung and during it all stand. It is not to be sung only by the cantor who intones it or by the choir, but by the whole of the people together.[5]

The Gospel Acclamation is not just an acclamation but also processional ritual music at its best. This music accompanies the procession of the Book of the Gospels to the ambo, where the gospel is proclaimed. The music should last as long as it takes to complete this action. The practice of repeating the acclamation after the gospel reading is certainly in keeping with the spirit of the liturgical moment.

GENERAL INTERCESSIONS

Also having roots in the Jewish synagogue, intercessory prayer is an important aspect of both Jewish and Christian worship. In the context of the Mass, the intercessions are also referred to as the "prayer of the faithful" because in the early church they took place after the catechumens were dismissed from the entire community. They take place now at the conclusion of the Liturgy of the Word, as a response to the proclaimed Word. The church offers its prayers for itself and for the needs of the world:

> Especially on Sundays and holy days of obligation there is to be restored, after the gospel and the homily, "the universal prayer" or "the prayer of the faithful." By this prayer, in which the people are to take part, intercession shall be made for holy Church, for the civil authorities, for those oppressed by various needs, for all people, and for the salvation of the entire world.[6]

Pastoral experience has shown that the intercessions often are dry and lifeless utterances. This is where musical presentation can help:

> Litanies are often more effective when sung. The repetition of melody and rhythm draws the people together in a strong and unified response…The general intercessions (prayer of the faithful) offer an opportunity for litanical singing.[7]

The intercessions should be petitionary in character and not statements of thanksgiving. We pray "for" the church, the poor, those who suffer from injustice. We do not pray for these people and organizations that they may conform to our agenda; rather, we offer them in prayer before God, with the fervent belief that God will respond. A good musical setting of the intercessions can help accomplish this either through a litanic, call-and-response version, or with an ongoing ostinato or mantra, with individual petitions offered, either sung or spoken over the repeated refrain.

When composing texts to be chanted or sung as the intercessions, remember these clear guidelines: Usually the prayers are for the church, for the world and those in leadership, for those who are experiencing injustice and for the needs of the local community. The texts should be brief and not too wordy.

TABLE

Although we do not know for certain, the Last Supper was probably a celebration of the Jewish Passover. This ancient celebration of freedom from slavery forms the basic outline for the Liturgy of the Eucharist in the Mass of the Roman Rite. The structure of taking bread, offering a prayer of blessing over bread and wine, and breaking, pouring and sharing of bread and cup form the basic elements of this ritual unit. While there have been many changes and adaptations throughout our liturgical history, this basic path of liturgical actions has remained the same.

The Liturgy of the Eucharist is truly an embodiment of a more individualistic piety for many, and music is one of many vehicles to help catechize and help people pull themselves into a more communal posture for these rites. The entire Liturgy of the Eucharist has a musical character, and the challenge for musicians is to help enable the unity of this part of the Mass to remain intact.

PREPARATION OF THE GIFTS

Formerly referred to as the "Offertory," the Preparation of the Gifts is exactly what its name says. During this time, the gifts of bread and wine are prepared, for the great offering, which is the Eucharistic Prayer. In other words, this rite is of secondary importance to what follows. The Preparation of the Gifts is a functional, transitional part of the ritual: The collection is gathered, the bread and wine are brought forward and prepared. There are many musical options to choose from at this point, but regardless of the choice, the duration of music should not exceed the ritual actions:

> The purpose of the rite is to prepare bread and wine for the sacrifice. The secondary character of the rite determines the manner of celebration.... The bringing of the gifts, the placing of the gifts on the altar, and the prayer over the gifts are primary. All else is secondary.[8]

> Song may accompany the procession and preparation of the gifts. It is not always necessary or desirable. Organ or instrumental music is also fitting at the time. When song is used, it need not speak of bread and wine or of offering. The proper function of this song is to accompany and celebrate the communal aspects of the procession. The text, therefore, can be any appropriate song or praise or rejoicing in keeping with the season.... Instrumental interludes can effectively accompany the procession and preparation of the gifts and thus keep this part of the Mass in proper perspective relative to the eucharistic prayer which follows.[9]

These guidelines are very helpful in understanding what this action is all about. The liturgical weight here is not as intense, and should not have much flourish or ceremony. This also offers the musician room for some creativity. Since the liturgical importance is lower at this point in the Mass, there are several options: instrumental music, solo or choral selection, or congregational hymn or song.

THE EUCHARISTIC PRAYER/EUCHARISTIC ACCLAMATIONS
(HOLY, HOLY; MEMORIAL ACCLAMATION; GREAT AMEN)

The origin of this prayer of blessing is the Jewish *berakah*. As Christianity grew, this prayer was adapted into many forms and styles, finally taking the present structure of the Eucharistic Prayer that we have today. The inner voice of the prayer is thanksgiving and praise: remembering God's saving action throughout history, in the present and in the kingdom that is to come. The prayer is truly a summary of life rooted in Jesus Christ.

Prior to Vatican II, there was for many generations only one approved form of the prayer. Now there are several prayers appearing in the sacramentary. The renewal of the council has helped us to remember that the prayer is not a solitary exercise of the presiding priest, but rather, the prayer of the entire gathered community:

> The eucharistic prayer, a prayer of thanksgiving and sanctification, is the center and high point of the entire celebration. In an introductory dialogue the priest invites the people to lift their hearts to God in prayer and thanks; he unites them with himself in the prayer he addresses in their name to the Father through Jesus Christ. The meaning of the prayer is that the whole congregation joins Christ in acknowledging the works of God and in offering the sacrifice.[10]

This important instruction suggests that the assembly is not an audience during this prayer, but active, passionate "co-celebrants" in the offering. That being the case, the implementation of music through the use of acclamations is critical, providing a vehicle in which the people rightfully participate:

> The acclamations are shouts of joy which arise from the whole assembly as forceful and meaningful assents....[11]

> The acclamations (...including the special acclamations of praise in the Eucharistic Prayers of Masses with Children) are the preeminent sung prayers of the eucharistic liturgy. Singing these acclamations makes their prayer all the more effective.[12]

The three important acclamations here are, of course, the Holy, Holy (Sanctus), the Memorial Acclamation and the concluding Doxology and Great Amen. Like other acclamatory moments in the liturgy, these three acclamations should be well known by the assembly, easily sung and capable eventually of being sung spontaneously by heart. Not only must they be accessible and singable, but these acclamations must remain vital and compelling for an assembly to sing over a period of time without changing settings. Also, because the unity of the entire prayer needs to be seen and respected, it is important that these three acclamations (and any additional ones) have a melodic unity. Music ministers should not mix and match these acclamations, but rather use them as a unit. They need to be big, strong, sturdy and to be given high priority in liturgical and musical weight.

The Eucharistic Prayer requires careful attention to be an effective prayer of thanksgiving and praise for our praying community and demands a place of priority in the planning and strategy making of parish musicians. Music has the potential to lift the prayer from being a priestly monologue to becoming a true communal experience.

THE LORD'S PRAYER

The Lord's Prayer is an ancient and most treasured prayer in every confession of Christianity throughout the world. The role of the prayer in the liturgy is that of communal invitation and preparation for communion. In other words, it is a communal prayer—always spoken or sung by the *entire* community. It is never to be implemented as a solo (which unfortunately happens too often, especially at wedding celebrations) or choral selection. It belongs to the assembly. That being the case, it is difficult to find a musical setting that everyone can easily participate in. The need for musicians and liturgists to consider the context of the prayer presents further complication. It should not overshadow the breaking of the bread and the sharing of Communion that follows. Given these two complications, reciting the prayer may be the most successful option. However, it can be sung as long as great care is taken to make sure it is a setting that the assembly can sing well, and one that is not overly dramatic, drawing too much attention to itself above the communal sharing of the meal that follows.

LAMB OF GOD

The Lamb of God accompanies the breaking and pouring of the bread and wine, and is one of the most ancient and traditional ritual moments found in the eucharistic liturgy. Like the acclamations during the Eucharistic Prayer, the Lamb of God should be sung and needs to musically "cover" the time and action of the breaking and pouring. This time (and the music that accompanies it) should not be rushed, and extra tropes can and should be added to build the momentum of this important liturgical action. There are many musical settings, and they work best when an effort is made to continue the music instrumentally under the priest's invitation to Communion, leading without interruption to the beginning of the communion song.

COMMUNION SONG

The sharing of the bread and wine by the assembly in solidarity with one another is the climactic ritual action of the Mass. This, again, is a communal action, not a time for individual piety or isolation. Great efforts are still needed to help our communities of faith grow in their understanding of this ritual moment. This is not private prayer alone with Jesus of Nazareth; this is a celebration of the Risen Lord, alive and present in our midst, and a call and challenge for all of us to become and live as the Body of Christ.

The communion song presents another occasion when there is a need for the community to sing. Unfortunately, in many parishes, these attempts at communal singing fail, and we resort to implementing either instrumental or solo or choral music, without the assembly's participation. We must not allow this practice to continue. To do so would be to violate the church's teaching and be in collusion with efforts to de-emphasize the communal nature and sharing of the Eucharist.

The first consideration is to follow the directives that instruct us to begin the song immediately after the "Lord, I am not worthy…." In fact, the music can begin instrumentally beneath the priest's invitation: "Behold the Lamb of God...." The sooner the communion song begins, the more opportunities for success. If the music ministers receive communion first and wait to begin the song after they are all back in place, then the silence or instrumental music during the first few communicants' reception will only encourage passivity and private piety. Begin the song as soon as possible. Also, choose one communion song only. Do not fill up the time with two or more pieces, which would only communicate the role of music as "filler." Find ways to extend the communion song through singing additional verses, or adding instrumental verses and interludes. The song should "cover" the entire action of the communion sharing:—*one* song—*one* message—*one* thought.

The type of song chosen is helpful in this regard. First, the text of the song should reflect what is happening. The message is not devotion but common sharing. Texts that speak to banquet and meal are the most appropriate and should be chosen above other texts. Second, choose songs that are not strophic-through composed, such as hymns. Find pieces that utilize a refrain accessible for the assembly that can be sung by heart, with the verses initially sung by the cantor or choir.

The role of the assembly during the sharing of Communion is in deep need of reform, and in addition to catechesis and preaching on this matter, the choice of music and deportment of musicians have great influence in helping us mature in our understanding of true Communion.

SONG OF PRAISE

Although it almost never occurs in a typical parish liturgy, the rubrics in the sacramentary and directives from other documents invite us to consider utilizing a communal song of praise after the silence that follows the sharing of Communion:

> After communion, the priest and people may spend some time in silent prayer. If desired, a hymn, or psalm or other song of praise may be sung by the entire congregation.[13]

> The singing of the psalm or hymn of praise after the distribution of communion is optional.... A congregational song may well provide a fitting expression of oneness in the Eucharistic Lord. Since no particular text is specified, there is ample room for creativity.[14]

These directives do *not* speak of the placement of a "meditation song" (an unfortunate practice that has become too prevalent), but a communal song of praise by the entire assembly, a response of thanks and gratitude to God for the gift of the Eucharist. It truly can be a wonderful way to unite the assembly and serve as a solution to the problem of the closing recessional song, which far too often becomes an opportunity to leave early and is perceived as "traveling" music for the priest as he leaves the worship space.

More parishes are using the option of a Song of Praise, with the assembly standing and singing a joyous and strong hymn, immediately followed by the prayer after Communion, the final blessing and dismissal. An adaptation of this practice is to sing a few stanzas of the hymn and then keep it going instrumentally, underpinning the prayer and final blessing. After the dismissal, the music could crescendo, and the priest and ministers could exit with the remaining stanzas. There is much room for creativity here.

GOING FORTH

Any communal gathering requires an element of closure and leave-taking, and the rite of going forth provides that movement. Musically, there are two ritual elements that can possibly be assisted with the use of music.

FINAL BLESSING

Though not required, music can be an option in a creative rendering of the final blessing. The more solemn blessings given in the sacramentary would lend themselves well to musical setting, either as *a cappella* chant or in more developed settings, with tropes either recited or sung by the presiding priest, followed by a common acclamatory response by the assembly.

SONG OF MISSION

The present Roman Rite Eucharist does not recommend or forbid a closing or recessional song; it does not refer to such a song at all. The common practice of a closing song is usually assumed, but our earlier discussion and examination of the optional use of a song of praise after Communion beg the question of what decision to make in regard to a closing song. As suggested earlier in this book, unfortunately, the closing song often is not experienced as a final song of mission or going forth, but rather, as an opportunity to grab coats and purses and scurry forth from the worship space.

When the option is suggested to not have a closing song as we usually experience it, people often respond by saying: "Well, if we do not have a song, the liturgy will not feel as though it is finished." This is an opportunity for us to reflect on the fact that, perhaps, the liturgy should *not* feel finished at all. The final words of the liturgy exhort the assembly to "go in peace to love and serve the Lord." Unfortunately, those words can get lost in a closing song. Perhaps a more open-ended closing of the ritual would help evangelize and help us to remember that the liturgy is truly a *dismissal* and to go forth from the worship event to true service and outreach.

Even if the decision is to have a closing song, be careful to choose songs with texts that truly reflect the missionary aspect of the entire liturgy. Look for texts that are strong, social-justice oriented, that focus on service, ministry and discipleship—the energies and challenges that compel us to gather in the first place. We come to worship in order to be strengthened and nurtured as a community so we can then be sent back into the world to be the presence of Jesus to the world, in word and in our living as the Body of Christ.

NOTES

[1] David Haas, copyright ©2001, The Emmaus Center for Music, Prayer and Ministry, Eagan, Minnesota 55122. Used with permission. All rights reserved.

[2] *Music in Catholic Worship,* n. 44.

[3] *Music in Catholic Worship,* n. 61.

[4] *Liturgical Music Today,* n. 18.

[5] National Conference of Catholic Bishops, *The Lectionary for Mass: Sundays, Solemnities, Feasts of the Lord and the Saints, Cycle C,* vol.1 (Collegeville, Minn.: The Liturgical Press, 2000), Introduction, n. 23.

[6] *The Constitution on the Sacred Liturgy,* n. 53.

[7] *Music in Catholic Worship,* n. 74.

[8] *Music in Catholic Worship,* n. 46.

[9] *Music in Catholic Worship,* n. 71.

[10] The General Instruction on the Roman Missal, n. 54.

[11] *Music in Catholic Worship,* n. 53.

[12] *Liturgical Music Today,* n. 17.

[13] The General Instruction on the Roman Missal, n. 56j.

[14] *Music in Catholic Worship,* n. 72.

CHAPTER EIGHT

THE LITURGICAL YEAR

Throughout all time I will sing to you. —David Haas[1]

WHEN MOST PEOPLE think of the liturgical year, what usually comes to mind are the tasks or admonitions associated with seasons, such as: "What color will we use for Advent this year?" or "Remember, we cannot sing 'Alleluia' during Lent" or "Can you use the organ on Good Friday?" Often people associate a discussion of the liturgical year with rules, directives and obligations.

This is most unfortunate because observation of the liturgical year can be experienced as very passionate, engaging and conversion-filled, one of the richest aspects of the church's liturgical life. In spite of our usual associations with the trappings of the liturgical year, this path of our worship life is indeed a powerful proclamation of mission. As an example, beneath the surface of the overflow of people attending Mass on Christmas Eve from a motive of nostalgia seeking, the carols and message of the sights and sounds of this season can truly arouse a hunger beyond a sense of obligation or a "stroll down memory lane." Christmas Eve is a time for the church to remember the message of "God with us." In other words, it celebrates God's fidelity to us to use all of creation to bear or give birth to the presence of God, "the Word made flesh."

So what is the liturgical year when viewed through the lens of mission and discipleship? The liturgical year is a single celebration, a strong and bold proclamation of the saving deeds of Jesus the Christ:

> The whole mystery of Christ, from his Incarnation to the day of Pentecost and the expectation of his coming again, is recalled by the Church during the course of the year.[2]

The liturgical year, while certainly counter to the civil or school calendar, should not compete with or be critical of the secular keeping of time. Neither should the church year be seen totally as a retrospective on the salvation of Christ already accomplished. The liturgical seasons provide a road map for envisioning a future in light of the saving acts of salvation history. Through the marking of time of seasons and feasts, the liturgical year is forward-looking in purpose, anticipating the final return of the Lord and proclaiming our need to be prepared for this coming.

Every element of the liturgical year is intrinsically tied to the mission and ministry of the church and to its communal prayer. What follows is a brief examination of these elements, which celebrate this understanding of the sanctification of time.

THE LECTIONARY

The guidebook for the liturgical year journey is the book of biblical texts that are chosen to be proclaimed at liturgies and celebrations throughout the year. Like the specific liturgical seasons, the presence of a lectionary originally was seen not as a straightjacket or set of limitations, but rather as a source to help propel the Christian community into mission and service. Some scholarship suggests that such an ordering of the Scriptures even preceded Jesus.

Contrasted with a more evangelical and fundamentalist approach to public proclamation of the Bible, in which the biblical text is sought after the message is determined, the ordering and structure of the lectionary actually determines the message. The lectionary keeps us from viewing the world through our own cultural biases and conditions. Instead, the lectionary offers us a discipline, a prepared way to enter the joys and mysteries of the story of salvation, from the God of the Covenant to the saving person of Jesus the Christ. The lectionary is freed from the limitations of human leaders.

Having origins probably in Jewish synagogues, the pattern of proclamation/preaching/practical application is a formula that is fundamental for believers. The lectionary patterns help us see and hear the gospel readings not as a play-by-play of the life of Jesus, but rather to express and share how the life of Jesus affected and changed the lives of all who experienced him. In addition to adding Gospel readings, one of the greatest steps forward in the renewal of the lectionary after the Second Vatican Council was the inclusion of a reading from the Old Testament. This inclusion changes the focus a bit in providing a historical and religious backdrop to the coming of the Messiah, so that we do not concentrate entirely on what Jesus said and did. This provides a religious and historical backdrop also to what happened to the people who were present when Jesus did the things he did and said the things he said, and, of course, what happens to us when we encounter this Word.

For instance, the Advent readings do more than just share the story of the events and times building up to the immediate coming of the historical Jesus. Rather, they compel us to reflect upon the reality that the promise of God has not been totally carried out, that God still has plans for us, and our task is to hope and wait with passion. Advent does much more than prepare for Christmas. It also prepares us for the final breaking forth of the reign of God in human history.

In the same way, Lent is not just a prelude to the Triduum (the three days: Holy Thursday, Good Friday and Easter); Lent is a proclamation of conversion and new life. The Easter Gospels are not just a retelling of the appearances of Jesus, but a pointing to the experience of what life in the Risen Christ can be for all.

The lectionary is a gift to the liturgical life of a community. Having an ordered pattern of the biblical texts offers a way in which we can hear and celebrate the Judeo-Christian story, not just in a step-by-step, chronological manner, but in a way that changes our lives forever with a response of service and discipleship.

The Sunday lectionary contains a three-year cycle of Scripture readings. Year A uses Gospel material mostly from Matthew, Year B utilizes Mark as its primary source and Year C celebrates the Good News through the lens of Luke's Gospel. All three of the years are supplemented with material from John's Gospel.

SUNDAY

In the New Testament, all four of the gospel evangelists speak about "the first day of the week" (see Matthew 28:1; Mark 16:9; Luke 24:1; John 20:1). It is on Sunday that Jesus appears to the disciples (see Matthew 28:9; Luke 24:13; John 20:19), Jesus shares the gifts of the Spirit (see Acts 2:1; John 20:22) and the disciples are sent on mission (see John 20:21–33; Acts 1:8; Acts 2:4). This "day of the Lord" is at the heart of the mission of Christ himself and is singled out as the day of the Resurrection. Psalm 118 also refers to "the day that the Lord has made" (verse 24), and Acts 20:7 speaks of early Christians gathered to "break bread" on the first day of the week.

Throughout church history, the keeping of Sunday as the time for Christians to gather for the liturgical meal was increasingly emphasized. Over the course of time, the Christian keeping of Sunday assumed the look of the Jewish Sabbath (beginning on Saturday). The early Christians, many of whom were Jewish, continued to observe their traditional Sabbath right alongside this new Christian celebration of Sunday. With the exception of the Eastern Orthodox, the rest of the church has held Sunday observance as a continuation of the original vision of Sabbath, as a time of rest to be reflective with the Word. Although many in Western culture (especially in the United States) have taken exception to the purity of the Sabbath as a time of rest, Sunday remains a different day for most. Sunday in most households is still a time to cultivate and nurture family and other important relationships, and a time to pursue more relaxing and recreational (non-work) activities. While work exerts an increasing amount of pressure on people and claims an increasing amount of people's time, the vision remains of Sabbath as a time of rest, contemplation and reflection, not as an obligation, but as an opportunity.

As for the early disciples, Sunday remains the primary time for the Christian community to gather and celebrate the presence of the Risen Christ. On Sunday we come together to call to mind his vision and teachings, and we believe that when we do so, he will be present: "For where two or three are gathered in my name, I am there among them" (Matthew 18:20).

In other words, when we meet on Sunday with the Resurrected One, we are experiencing an encounter with the living Christ. We gather primarily not to teach or learn about Jesus, but to meet him. We gather not only to praise God, but also and more fundamentally to be formed by the Word. When we surrender to be formed by that Word, we will be able to praise God more authentically. We gather not to be with friends and other people we like, but we come together to be joined as the Body of Christ—this Christ who brings us together. Catechesis, praise and fellowship flow from our experience together, but are not the central intent of our gathering. Rather, our purpose is to celebrate the presence of the crucified and resurrected Lord.

Because the community repeatedly gathers together on this day on when the resurrected Lord appeared, the Sunday worshipping community is a proclamation of the presence of Jesus, who has died and rose, in the here and now. This makes discipleship possible and important. Every resurrection appearance in the Gospels begins with a group of terrified, confused and disillusioned disciples huddled together and paralyzed by fear, shame and grief. Jesus appears with Good News: Death is no longer the dominating power in our lives, and it is replaced with the proclamation of victory over suffering, pain and hopelessness:

When it was evening on that day, the first day of the week, and the doors of the house where the disciples had met were locked for fear of the Jews, Jesus came and stood among them and said, "Peace be with you." *(John 20:19)*

But the story does not end there. Jesus is always about sending his followers out from the gathering, out from the comfort zone of meal and friendship, to real mission, proclaiming reconciliation and the call to serve:

Then he opened their minds to understand the scriptures, and he said to them, "Thus it is written, that the Messiah is to suffer and to rise from the dead on the third day, and that repentance and forgiveness of sins is to be proclaimed in his name to all nations, beginning from Jerusalem. You are witnesses of these things…." *(Luke 24:45-48)*

As ministers of the liturgy, we need to nurture this sense of "the first day of the week" as more than a nostalgic acting out of what Jesus did, but, more importantly, an urging of the community to reach out in action. In our pastoral efforts, we should do more than enforce the primacy of Sunday, but catechize and help our communities discover the riches held in taking time to be attentive to the presence of the Risen Lord.

THE PASCHAL CYCLE: LENT, TRIDUUM, EASTER

Like Sunday, the primacy of Easter in our liturgical life and mission in faith is foundational. Originally, this central celebration was called *Pasch,* from the Greek word for Passover. This linkage of Passover to the Sunday eucharistic gathering comes from the events that surrounded Jesus at that last meal of his earthly ministry, including his farewell, incarceration, crucifixion and death, and his resurrection, ascension and the sending of the Holy Spirit. This is only one of many Jewish festivals that became "christianized." Here the "new Passover" extends beyond the dramatic story of the Red Sea, but transforms into an all-night sharing of stories and songs of God's liberation, centering on the Paschal Mystery of Jesus (betrayal, crucifixion, death and resurrection). This celebration always concluded with an early morning sharing of bread and wine. As the Jewish calendar became less of a focus for the early Gentile Christians, Sunday then became the regular day of celebration.

It is in the context of these early celebrations of Easter that baptism became a focus of the season. This vision is given to us in the New Testament, and proclaimed at the Easter Vigil:

Do you not know that all of us who have been baptized into Christ Jesus were baptized into his death? Therefore we have been buried with him by baptism into death, so that, just as Christ was raised from the dead by the glory of the Father, we too might walk in newness of life. For if we have been united with him in a death like his, we will certainly be united with him in a resurrection like his. We know that our old self was crucified with him so that the body of sin might be destroyed, and we might no longer be enslaved to sin. For whoever has died is freed from sin. But if we have died with Christ, we believe that we will also live with him. We know that Christ, being raised from the dead, will never die again; death no longer has dominion over him. The death he died, he died to sin, once for all; but the life he lives, he lives to God. So you also must consider yourselves dead to sin and alive to God in Christ Jesus. *(Romans 6:3–11)*

Paul's understanding of baptism as a dying with Christ, joined by the promise of rising again, is an important link. This connection with Christian initiation and the passion and resurrection of Jesus has remained to this day. Baptism truly is a celebration of moving through death to life, ending one way of life and embracing a new path. These new believers became part of the faith community not through learning new formulas or improving their moral life; they did so by dying as slaves and choosing to be reborn into new freedom.

Very early on, the church, together with the catechumens (those seeking initiation) and penitents (those seeking reconnections and reconciliation with the community), mark time on the journey of Lent. In addition to standing in solidarity with those on the margins, the entire Christian community has always seen Lent as a retreat, a time of ongoing spiritual growth and renewal. Lent is a process, a journey, a time of conversion, but more than these a movement to "hurry up slowly." The work of conversion and transformation takes time, and the church takes these forty days intentionally and deliberately to focus on the themes of movement and metanoia. The well-known disciplines of Lent (fasting, praying and the giving of alms) become useful tools and vehicles for growth in faith. Unfortunately, we tend to see these practices in minimal terms. Fasting, for instance, was never intended to be about "giving up things." Fasting meant an intent to be identified with the person of Jesus, to be given for the sake of others. These disciplines are more richly an opportunity for rededication of ourselves to the mission of Christ.

If we dare to look at its power and message, the celebration of the Triduum has the potential to be dangerous, if we only see it as a dramatic event that took place a long time ago, very far away and that happened to someone else. These intense three days (Holy Thursday, Good Friday and Easter) are not commemorations of past events. To be lulled into this shallow understanding is to believe that Jesus only was present in first-century Palestine. Jesus is present in the here and now. Any dramatization of the past has to balance with a passionate proclamation and sharing of the present story of Christ moving in the midst of human vessels in the everyday life of the faith community. The central event of the Triduum is that the terror and liberation of Jesus' journey is shared by all.

The Paschal Mystery is the central story of our lives—and for music ministers, this cannot be seen more clearly than in the musical proclamation of the Exsultet, the great Easter song that begins the Easter Vigil. Throughout this profound text, we hear over and over again the images that identify this night as the true Passover:

This is our passover feast,
> when Christ, the true Lamb is slain,
> whose blood consecrates the homes of all believers.

This is the night when first you saved our fathers:
> you freed the people of Israel from their slavery
> and led them dry-shod through the sea.

This is the night when the pillar of fire
 destroyed the darkness of sin!

This is the night when Christians everywhere,
 washed clean of sin
 and freed from all defilement,
 are restored to grace and grow together in holiness.

This is the night when Jesus Christ
 broke the chains of death
 and rose triumphant from the grave.[3]

With this proclamation, we celebrate that we ourselves are carried through death to life, not in the past, but now in the present. Christ reigns and conquers death *now*. For ministers of music, this text celebrates the hope of all humanity and the assurance of liberation in the here and now. This affirmation and profession of faith is central to the earliest understandings of Easter and, more intensely, for those seeking initiation and for the ongoing rebirth of all the baptized. This profound story of what it means to be Christian is the central and most powerful metaphor in our faith life, and needs to be embraced for those of us who lead communities in sung prayer.

THE INCARNATION CYCLE: ADVENT, CHRISTMAS

The journey of this season, which begins on the First Sunday of Advent, and concludes with the celebration of the Baptism of the Lord, is a series of festivals that are powerful and, of course, very familiar. There are many theories about the origins of Christmas, but most agree that its roots are found in cosmology. Christmas utilizes cosmological images as audiovisual tools, proclaiming a wonderful image of the Incarnation. The days during this time start to last a bit longer, the sun rises higher and, while we know that winter will last a while, we see that light and life are not absent, but renewed with vigor. These images work profoundly with the new brightness and renewal that come to and with the birth of Christ, the true light of the world. Winter may become more fierce, but the Son of God is truly like the sun: glorious and victorious. Once again, we see a pagan festival become "christianized" (in this case, the ancient Roman festival of Saturnalia), but it would be shallow to limit this "christianization" to a mere borrowing from a different culture and belief system. Christmas also developed as a response to heresy in the solar festival's teaching about the Incarnation. But that pales dramatically in comparison to the celebration of the birth of Jesus as the celebration of the very presence of the Word of God.

Advent is more than a preparation and celebration of the coming of Jesus in history—it is a bold and passionate trumpet blast, proclaiming the eternal promise of God's covenant. Jesus will truly come again, in our history, in our hearts and in our ultimate destiny. Again, there are many developments historically that led to a season of Advent, but it has always had an important two-tiered focus:

The season of Advent has a twofold character. It is a time of preparation for Christmas when the first coming of God's Son...[i]s recalled. It is also a season when minds are directed by this memorial to Christ's second coming at the end of time. It is thus a season of joyful and spiritual expectation.[4]

In other words, Advent is not a mini-Lent or a penitential season at all, but a focused, joyful sojourn of hope of the fulfillment of salvation history. For ministers of music, it is important to ensure that this twofold focus remains vibrant, especially the hope that arises to passionate waiting in faith. This is profoundly proclaimed in the wonderful hymn, "Each Winter As the Year Grows Older":

Each winter as the year grows older,
We each grow older too.
The chill sets in a little colder;
The verities we knew seem shaken and untrue.

When race and class cry out for treason,
When sirens call for war,
They overshout the voice of reason,
And scream till we ignore all we held dear before.

Yet I believe beyond believing,
That life can spring from death;
That growth can flower from our grieving;
That we can catch our breath and turn transfixed by faith.

So even as the sun is turning,
To journey to the north,
The living flame, in secret burning,
Can kindle on the earth, and bring God's love to birth.

O child of ecstasy and sorrows,
O Prince of peace and pain,
Brighten today's world by tomorrow's,
Renew our lives again; Lord Jesus, come again.[5]

Advent is the season of hope and a new vision of the world and how we live, and for music ministers, the song is one of justice and peace, embodied in the words of the Magnificat:

All that I am sings of the God
Who brings new life to birth in me.
My spirit soars on the wings of my Lord.

My soul gives glory to the Lord,
Rejoicing in my saving God,
Who looks upon me in my state
And all the world will call me blest;
For God works marvels in my sight,
And holy, holy is God's name!

God's mercy is from age to age,
On those who follow in fear;
Whose arm is power and strength
And scatters all the proud of heart;
Who casts the mighty from their thrones
And raises up the lowly ones!

God fills the starving with good things,
The rich are left with empty hands;
Protecting all the faithful ones,
Remembering Israel with mercy,
The promise known to those before
And to their children forever! *(Rory Cooney, text, ©GIA)*[6]

Christmas is more than just a remembrance of the historical birth of Christ, but a wonderful celebration of mission and social action. It is more than the surface example of the Magi bringing gifts to the Christ Child—it is an example of God, who gives us the very gift of the Christ Child himself! The wonderful and well-known Christmas story by Charles Dickens, *A Christmas Carol*, is a challenge to all of this—that our recognition of and conversion to the Incarnation compels us to be in service to the poor, both in our present attitudes and in outreach and action. Christmas is a season of secular consumerism and hectic craziness, and all who long for liberation and community look to the Christ Child and find him in the simple joys of common attentiveness and service to those in pain and need:

Star-Child, earth-Child,
go-between of God,
love child, Christ Child,
heaven's lightning rod:

Street child, beat child,
no place left to go,
hurt child, used child
no one wants to know:

Grown child, old child,
mem'ry full of years,

sad child, lost child,
story told in tears:

Spared child, spoiled child,
having, wanting more,
wise child, faith child
knowing joy in store:

Hope-for-peace Child,
God's stupendous sign,
down-to-earth Child,
Star of stars that shine:

> This year, this year let the day arrive
> when Christmas comes for everyone,
> everyone alive![7]

ORDINARY TIME AND SPECIAL FEASTS

The term "Ordinary Time" is most unfortunate because there is nothing ordinary about these times at all. In the lectionary, Ordinary Time consists of the time after Epiphany and another time after Pentecost. It is during this time that we have a more semi-continuous reading of the Scripture—a particular book of the Bible is read through, with some intentional exceptions and omissions.

It is during Ordinary Time that the Paschal Mystery is more developed. It is this breaking open of the central mystery of death and resurrection that brings the centralities of our faith into focus.

In the midst of this time, the church celebrates important feasts that originally began as responses to certain pieties and devotions and then developed into liturgical celebrations in their own right. These celebrations provide for us a focus on certain key aspects of the Christian journey and faith and provide opportunity for deeper contemplation into these mysteries. Three examples will be explored briefly.

Trinity Sunday, on the Sunday after Pentecost, can be seen as a celebration of thanksgiving of salvation history and provides a celebration of theology through its recognition of salvation as being completed and accomplished by the Father through the Son and in the Holy Spirit. The images in this feast are filled with metaphors of praise, providing the believer with a touchstone for that praise.

The Solemnity of the Body and Blood of Christ (Corpus Christi) was originally connected to a period in history (the twelfth century) in which there was a strong emphasis on the Blessed Sacrament. The special emphasis on the real presence in the already consecrated bread led to the development of this solemnity. The liturgical practice of the elevated host and eucharistic processions came directly from this movement. However, it is important to note that the real saving event is the great prayer of thanksgiving and the common sharing of the eucharistic banquet, and other practices should take second place in our planning and in our attitudes. Regardless of its origins, this celebration provides a time to revel in and reverence the prominence of the Eucharist in our lives. Beyond the consecration of the human objects of bread and wine, indicating a eucharistic theology embodying our call to be bread broken and wine poured out for the life of the world.

The liturgy of Christ the King is the most recent of those feasts honoring Jesus Christ, instituted officially in the early twentieth century as a response to the destructive forces of the age and culture—leading toward a pastoral need seen at the time, to acknowledge the kingship of Christ. This liturgy is probably more authentically celebrated within the other seasons of the year (such as Advent, Christmas, Epiphany, Easter and Ascension), but can be seen and celebrated as an intensifying of the kerygma that we celebrate every Sunday: Jesus Christ is Lord!

THE MISSION OF THE LITURGICAL YEAR

The liturgical year is a wonderful resource for the Christian faith. We have this ordering not to teach a mere formula of time, but rather to challenge the Christian community to join Christ in his mission in obedience to God and to help renew the face of the earth. The seasons of the church year are proclamations of God revealed to the world, and provide a structure in which God can be present to us in a compelling way. Just like creation changes in weather, in the phases of the stars and planets, and in the rising and setting of the sun, the liturgical year marks the passionate ways in which God hopes to speak to us. This system of time proclaims that God is present in the ordinary, the everyday and in the ebb and flow of life. Bottom line, keeping it helps our God not seem so remote, but powerfully and intimately invested in us and in our destiny. Through the sounds and sonorities of our music and sung prayer, we music ministers help provide a vehicle for this most wonderful mystery.

NOTES

[1] David Haas, "Throughout All Time," copyright ©1998, GIA Publications. All rights reserved.

[2] General Norms for the Liturgical Year and the Calendar, n. 17; cf. *The Constitution on the Sacred Liturgy*, 102.

[3] The Exsultet, from the Easter Vigil, the Sacramentary/Roman Missal.

[4] General Norms for the Liturgical Year, n. 39.

[5] William and Annabeth Gay, "Each Winter as the Year Grows Older," copyright ©1971, United Church Press. All rights reserved.

[6] Rory Cooney, "Magnificat," copyright ©1991, GIA Publications. All rights reserved.

[7] Shirley Erena Murray, "Star-Child," copyright ©1994, Hope Publishing Company. All rights reserved.

CHAPTER NINE

PREPARING FOR THE LITURGY—RESOURCES AND PROCESS

Prepare the way of the Lord. —*Matthew 3:3*

GOOD LITURGY WITH MUSIC well integrated into the ritual does not just happen. While room must be made for the Spirit to weave its magic, this weaving must take place within a structure and design that is well thought through and prepared. This book has repeatedly emphasized the need for music ministers to be well-versed in liturgy. In addition, whether or not music ministers are part of an ongoing liturgy planning team, or on their own in their preparation process, planning must take place.

As we have seen, a parish music minister needs to be skilled and knowledgeable in the liturgy and have basic competence in how liturgical music functions and how music is situated within the context of ritual action. Music ministers also need to keep abreast of the latest repertoire and stay connected to professional organizations and developments in the field. What follows is a listing of basic resources and helpful guides.

RITUAL BOOKS

Every minister of music who is charged with choosing and preparing music for the liturgy should have the following ritual books as primary reference materials. Most of these ritual books are available from various publishers, and many are published in study editions as well.

ESSENTIAL RITUAL TEXTS

THE SACRAMENTARY
THE LECTIONARY

LECTIONARY FOR MASSES WITH CHILDREN
RITE OF CHRISTIAN INITIATION OF ADULTS
RITE OF BAPTISM FOR CHILDREN
RITE OF MARRIAGE
ORDER OF CHRISTIAN FUNERALS
RITE OF PENANCE
PASTORAL CARE OF THE SICK: RITES OF ANOINTING AND VIATICUM
RITE OF HOLY COMMUNION AND WORSHIP OF THE EUCHARIST OUTSIDE MASS
SUNDAY CELEBRATIONS IN THE ABSENCE OF A PRIEST
RITES OF RELIGIOUS PROFESSION: PASTORAL INTRODUCTION AND COMPLETE TEXT
BOOK OF BLESSINGS
CATHOLIC HOUSEHOLD BLESSINGS AND PRAYERS

LITURGICAL DOCUMENTS AND PASTORAL RESOURCES

In addition to the sacramentary, the lectionary and other ritual books, there are many important and helpful documents, books and resources. There are too many to mention, but what follows are some strong and basic recommendations for ongoing education, formation, reflection and evaluation in your ministry.

THE LITURGY DOCUMENTS: A PARISH RESOURCE
Volumes One and Two, David A. Lysik and Frederick R. McManus, editors,
Chicago: Liturgy Training Publications, 1991

Contained in these two volumes are the most critical documents and guidelines for music ministers and all involved in liturgical ministry, including the two fundamental documents for music, *Music in Catholic Worship* and *Liturgical Music Today*, both from the Bishops' Committee on the Liturgy. Other key documents included are *The General Instruction on the Roman Missal, Environment and Art in Catholic Worship* and *The Directory for Masses With Children*. These and other documents in these volumes articulate the theology, vision and norms for liturgical celebration. This resource is a must.

THE MILWAUKEE SYMPOSIA FOR CHURCH COMPOSERS: A TEN YEAR REPORT
Chicago: Liturgy Training Publications, 1992

The Symposia was an ongoing gathering of composers, liturgists and pastoral ministers who gathered regularly to reflect upon issues regarding the state of liturgical music. This document summarizes their discussions and reflections, and offers a follow-up to the issues raised and articulated in *Music in Catholic Worship*. Topics addressed here include: music as a language of faith, liturgical formation and preparation, liturgical and musical structures, textual considerations, cross-cultural music making, models of musical leadership, technology and worship and the musical-liturgical-pastoral judgment.

DAVID HAAS, *MUSIC AND THE MASS: A GUIDE FOR MINISTERS OF MUSIC*
Chicago: Liturgy Training Publications, 1998

A walk-through of every ritual moment of the liturgy, this book provides biblical sources, liturgical documentation and other historical and pastoral notes for all of the actions of the liturgy. A special commentary directed toward the music minister concludes each section. For those finding it difficult to wade through all of the liturgical documents, this resource offers summaries and a synthesis of that material, with an emphasis on pastoral implementation.

SOURCEBOOK FOR SUNDAYS AND SEASONS: AN ALMANAC OF PARISH LITURGY
Chicago: Liturgy Training Publications, annual

This annual publication is a goldmine of help and a must for all involved in liturgy and music preparation. It provides notes for preparation, music and ritual suggestions, sample texts, important seasonal information and creative ideas for the liturgical year.

LIVING LITURGY: SPIRITUALITY, CELEBRATION AND CATECHESIS FOR SUNDAYS AND SOLEMNITIES
Collegeville, Minn.: The Liturgical Press, annual

A wonderful annual resource, this work contains not only helpful biblical insights for each Sunday, but offers many pastoral touchstones for the various liturgical ministries. A unique aspect is focus on the spiritual, liturgical and catechetical aspects of a specific celebration. This is an excellent resource for both musicians and liturgists.

GABE HUCK, *LITURGY WITH STYLE AND GRACE*
Chicago: Liturgy Training Publications, 1984

This excellent book on the basics provides an overview of the central rituals: the celebration of the Mass, the sacraments and the seasons of the liturgical year.

AUSTIN FLEMING, *PREPARING FOR LITURGY*
Chicago: Liturgy Training Publications, 1997

All liturgical planners should read and reread this book in order to understand the psychology and dynamics in the liturgical preparation process. Father Fleming draws from a strong theological background and years of pastoral experience. This book embraces a process and philosophy that all parish communities should embrace.

JAN MICHAEL JONCAS, *THE CATECHISM OF THE CATHOLIC CHURCH ON LITURGY AND SACRAMENTS*
San Jose, Calif.: Resource Publications, 1995

Since the new catechism raises important questions and issues regarding our liturgical and sacramental life, this little book helps clarify the teachings regarding worship.

BERNARD HUIIJBERS, *THE PERFORMING AUDIENCE*
Portland, Ore.: Pastoral Press/Oregon Catholic Press, 1974

Excellent but little known, this is a foundational resource for understanding the theology and methodology of ritual music.

JOHN BELL, *THE SINGING THING: A CASE FOR CONGREGATIONAL SONG*
Chicago: GIA Publications, Inc., 2001
An "unapologetically anecdotal" presentation by a true master of congregational song.

PAUL WESTERMEYER, *THE HEART OF THE MATTER*
Chicago: GIA Publications, Inc., 2001
This little book is a wonderful exploration of images and a sound theology of liturgical music. Easy to read, but filled with depth.

LUCIEN DEISS, *VISIONS OF LITURGY AND MUSIC FOR A NEW CENTURY*
Collegeville, Minn.: The Liturgical Press, 1996
This is a rich resource of liturgical theology and biblical sources for those interested in digging deeper into the historical sources of liturgical music.

JAN MICHAEL JONCAS, *FROM SACRED SONG TO RITUAL MUSIC: TWENTIETH-CENTURY UNDERSTANDINGS OF ROMAN CATHOLIC WORSHIP MUSIC*
Collegeville, Minn.: The Liturgical Press, 1997
Exploring both theory and practice in regard to liturgical music theology, this work holds a comparative analysis of official and other important documents. This is an excellent resource to explore the various commentaries on pastoral liturgical music practice.

IRENE NOWELL, *SING A NEW SONG: THE PSALMS IN THE SUNDAY LECTIONARY*
Collegeville, Minn.: The Liturgical Press, 1993
This one-of-a-kind resource examines the psalms as they appear and are appointed in the Sunday lectionary. Truly a treasure for all who want to dig deeper into the spiritual, biblical and liturgical viewpoint of the Psalter, this work provides rich connections for music directors and cantors.

PEGGY LOVREIN, *THE LITURGICAL MUSIC ANSWER BOOK*
San Jose, Calif.: Resource Publications, Inc., 1999
A great resource, dealing with many issues that affect music ministers. Question-and-answer format.

HYMNALS AND OTHER MUSICAL RESOURCES

There are many resources available to the parish music minister. While any listing of hymnals, songbooks and other musical resources becomes dated and new resources are continually being published, I would strongly recommend that you add the following resources alongside the ritual books on your shelf.

RITUAL SONG: A HYMNAL AND SERVICE BOOK FOR ROMAN CATHOLICS
Chicago: GIA Publications, Inc., 1996
This complete and balanced service book is from the wonderful family of GIA hymnals, containing a balance of repertoire of many styles, along with ritual music for various rites, a complete liturgical Psalter, new creative approaches in ritual music and excellent indices.

GATHER COMPREHENSIVE

Chicago: GIA Publications, Inc., 1994

The entire contents of *Gather Second Edition,* plus 250 hymns and music from the traditional repertoire, are to be found in this resource. Containing music primarily in the contemporary genre, this work includes several complete Mass settings, a Psalter based on the three-year liturgical cycle and music representing many publishers and composers.

WORSHIP THIRD EDITION

Chicago: GIA Publications, Inc., 1997

This classic, well-known hymnal represents the best in classical hymnody, psalmody and ritual music.

WORD AND SONG

Schiller Park, Ill.: World Library Publications, annual

Featuring the best music published primarily by World Library composers, this hymnal offers a wonderful collection of ritual music and music selections for children. This annual collection is highly recommended for those utilizing the music from the catalog of World Library.

LEAD ME, GUIDE ME

Chicago: GIA Publications, Inc., 1987

A one-of-a-kind resource, *Lead Me, Guide Me,* contains the best of traditional and contemporary music from the African American tradition, most of it very difficult to find in print elsewhere. This is a must for your shelf of resources.

FLOR Y CANTO

Portland, Ore.: Oregon Catholic Press Publications, 1989

This is an important resource for the best of music from the Hispanic community. Many pieces are in Spanish and English.

SINGING OUR FAITH

Chicago: GIA Publications, 2001

This basic hymnal/prayer book for grade school students in Catholic schools may be used also in a parish religious education program. The accompanying leader's guide is a rich and important resource for implementing prayer with children.

GLORY AND PRAISE

Portland, Ore.: Oregon Catholic Press, 1997

This hymnal of music, primarily contemporary in style with some inclusion of popular hymnody, features the best of the Oregon Catholic Press composers.

PSALMS FOR THE CHURCH YEAR (IN SEVERAL VOLUMES)

Chicago: GIA Publications

This is an ongoing series of responsorial psalm settings, composed by Marty Haugen, David Haas, Rory Cooney, Gary Daigle, John Foley, Malcolm Kogut, the Dameans and others.

SINGING THE PSALMS

Portland, Ore.: Oregon Catholic Press, 1995

Another ongoing series of psalm settings for use throughout the liturgical year, this one features composers such as Christopher Walker, Bob Hurd, Bernadette Farrell, Jaime Cortez and others.

DAVID HAAS, *WHO CALLS YOU BY NAME: MUSIC FOR CHRISTIAN INITIATION*

Chicago: GIA Publications, 1991

This is an ongoing series of music resources for the various rites of Christian initiation, especially the rites for adults. Special emphasis is placed on ritual music and acclamations for the various ritual celebrations.

BLEST ARE THEY WHO MOURN

Chicago: GIA Publications, 1993

This is a diverse musical and liturgical resource for celebrating the various funeral rites, based on the new Order of Christian Funerals. Included with the many musical selections and ideas are a people's edition, a vigil booklet and vigil cards providing various options for pastoral settings.

PRAISE GOD IN SONG

Chicago: GIA Publications, 1979

For parishes wanting to begin celebrating morning and evening prayer in the parish this is a fundamental resource. Several settings are included which model good celebration and foundations for adaptation.

WHEN LOVE IS FOUND: A WEDDING LITURGY PREPARATION RESOURCE

Chicago: GIA Publications, 1993

This is a complete musical and liturgical resource for all involved in the planning of wedding celebrations, including a workbook for couples, and editions for the cantor and choir, as well as for the presider. Included are new settings of psalms, hymns, songs and ritual music for the marriage rites.

Obviously, this is only a partial list of the unending number of resources that are available to the parish musician. Music ministry leaders should always keep themselves abreast of the many existing and new collections being published, and keep themselves on the mailing lists of the major liturgical publishers.

In addition to the above resources, there are several quarterly magazines that make musical suggestions for liturgical seasons and feasts. Such resources are helpful, but they cannot and should not replace a prayerful and pastoral process with considerations needed to prepare a liturgy for a specific community or event.

A PROCESS FOR LITURGICAL PREPARATION

It is important to remember that the liturgy is already planned. Its structure is already in place and does not need or require manipulation on our part. The beginning elements are there. We need only to shape and *prepare* these elements, to fine-tune and focus the ritual patterns that are before us. Preparing a liturgy is more than filling in slots on a form, or picking out songs. Quality and responsible liturgical preparation require that the entire ritual experience be examined, identifying the key ritual moments, actions, gestures, sounds and other attitudes that will engage the community in an authentic and vibrant experience.

It is also good to focus our thinking about who should be part of the liturgy preparation process. There are two types of liturgical planning: (1) seasonal and long-range planning, and (2) planning for a specific liturgical celebration. Many parishes have a liturgy or worship committee, which is an important and vital group to have in place to direct the vision of the parish's liturgical life and to evaluate and plan for the future. This committee can and, in my estimation, should be engaged in the long-range planning for seasonal principles and priorities. Such a committee, however, is not necessarily the group that should prepare a specific liturgy. The parish liturgy committee, in my opinion, is a larger group of people, concerned with the overall liturgical and prayer life of the community, and is more of a visionary group. Their job lies in setting liturgical policies, setting the tone for and evaluating major feasts and seasons, and offering more general direction to the parish staff and community at large.

I would propose that a smaller, more focused group be engaged in the actual nuts and bolts of liturgical planning. While it may not always be possible, this group should include at least one of the priests who will preside at the parish liturgies, the music director, or someone deputized and competent to make suggestions and decisions on their behalf and, if there is one, a liturgist. In addition to these people (who may be full-time, part-time or volunteer parish staff), there should be two or three people from the community at large who represent a cross section of the parish, and who are properly formed to do the task. Basically we are talking about a group of five or six people at most. It is desirable that this group make an ongoing commitment to this ministry of preparation, meeting regularly and developing a connection with each other and to their task. It is best if they engage themselves in the study of the liturgy and sharpen their knowledge and skills in the process of preparing liturgical experiences.

Whenever possible, the priest should be present at this meeting because his role is obviously a central part of the entire liturgical experience. In many pastoral settings, however, the priest is not able to participate. Even in this case some adaptation of this process should be in place, at least for those making musical choices.

There are some basic materials for the meeting, including a lectionary, the sacramentary and the parish hymnal or music resource, and before the actual preparation begins, some grounding questions should be considered:

What are the conditions under which this celebration will take place?
Who will be there—age groups, cultural groupings, economic distinctions?
What are the "clash of the calendar" issues (for example, Pentecost vs. Memorial Day, Sunday in Easter vs. Mother's Day, Catechetical or Vocation Sunday)?
What is going on in the lives of the parish community, in the country, in the world?

After grappling with these and other important questions, then a more focused process can begin. What follows is a sketch of a ten-step, prayerful process that I have found helpful in preparing specific liturgical celebrations.

1. PREPARE FOR THE MEETING

Prior to the meeting, members of the team take time to read and pray over the Scriptures for the upcoming celebration, and perhaps read a commentary on those readings.

2. BEGIN WITH PRAYER (INCLUDING SILENCE)

3. EVALUATE THE PREVIOUS SUNDAY OR CELEBRATION

Evaluation is important and should not be overlooked. Good notes should be taken, and honest and forthright reflection can be helpful. This should not take up too much of the time of the meeting, but it should not be ignored.

4. START WITH THE SCRIPTURE

- A member of the team carefully and prayerfully reads the Gospel selection for the celebration. The rest of the team listens (no taking notes) reflectively. The other team members do *not* follow along in their missalettes or lectionary—listening and experiencing the reading is the focus. Try not to become task oriented at this point, but treat yourselves to drinking in the richness of the Word. This is reflective listening.

- A good intentional silence follows (with no note taking).

- A *different* member of the team then reads the same Gospel selection again. This time other members of the team take notes, focusing on key and striking phrases or images heard in the reading. These are *not* notes about which songs to use, or anything else related to the specific task, rather, the focus of the reflection here is: What in the reading is coming to the surface of our hearts and minds on a *faith* level?

- Again, a good intentional silence follows.

- Discussion and faith sharing then begin among team members. Again, the temptation is to go right to filling in the blanks, shouting out song ideas and so on. Try to avoid this at this point. Stay at the level of faith sharing.

- Repeat the same process with the First Reading (usually from the Old Testament). The first reading usually has a strong connection to the Gospel reading.

- As with the Gospel reading, discussion of or faith sharing on this reading can take place, along with drawing connections and pointing out similarities found in the Gospel reading. Share those connections, and now begin to develop a focus (not a theme) found in the Scriptures. At this point a good commentary can be helpful because it is important to have some grasp of the original intent of the biblical authors. This cannot be reduced to "what I think the Scripture means." This understanding can be corrective when we reflect on the pastoral dimensions of the Word.

- Members of the team then read the Second Reading and the text of the proper Responsorial Psalm for that liturgy. Sometimes the connections of these texts with the Gospel are strong; sometimes they are not.

- At this point, the personal faith sharing of the team should change its focus to that of the community who will celebrate this ritual. One question that should begin to arise at this point is: What are these Scriptures attempting to proclaim to the church at large and to this community of faith? This process is forming the basis for homily content.

5. LOOK AT SOME OF THE OTHER RITUAL TEXTS

The team then should look at the opening prayer (collect) of the particular celebration. This usually affirms the focus found in the Word. The same is true for the Communion Antiphon, the Prayer Over the Gifts and the Prayer after Communion. These texts are often ignored, and they provide a richness that can truly reveal the focus of the celebration.

6. REVEAL THE RELATIONSHIP TO THE SEASON

Consider how the biblical and ritual texts appointed for this liturgy relate to the specific or overall liturgical season.

7. BE ATTENTIVE TO THE SPECIFIC RITUAL UNITS FOUND IN THE LITURGY

GATHERING

Since the gathering rites are intended to form a diverse group of people into a prayerful and attentive community, the team needs to reflect on how the beginning of the celebration can help to embody the focus and intent of the Word. Is the mood joyful or somber, thankful or penitential in nature? Do pieces of music begin to come to mind? What ritual creativity is possible? Decisions regarding use of the Penitential Rite, Gloria and Sprinkling need to be made here, and questions around the ritual choreography need to be made. Will there be a procession? What are the primary symbols?

WORD

Go back to the Liturgy of the Word and consider, how should the community respond to what it has heard? Should there be a recitation of the creed, or should it be dropped? Should intercessions be sung or recited? Are we tying in the message of the Word into the content of these intentions? What about the Gospel acclamation? Would a procession of the Book of the Gospels be appropriate? Should we use incense during the acclamation? Other creative ritual questions: How can the homily be more participatory with the assembly? How about a sung refrain during the homily, attempting to echo the message in the preaching? These and other related issues should be discussed.

TABLE

Which Eucharistic Prayer text would be most suitable for the occasion? What preface best echoes the Word for this celebration? Should the prayer be sung? Should the Preparation of the Gifts be simple, or more elaborate? What song would best accompany the sharing of Communion? Again, a choice that is focused on meal-sharing, but at the same time supports the message of the Word is best. These are some of the many decisions that should be made about these rites.

GOING FORTH

The main considerations here are: How are we sending the community forth to more deeply live out the Word proclaimed and preached today? How can the meal that has been shared be embodied by our considerations of the final blessing, or a song of sending forth?

8. BEGIN TO MAKE SPECIFIC CHOICES AND TIGHTEN UP LOOSE ENDS

This can take a variety of forms. Some final details can be settled here at the meeting, or after the meeting concludes. In most cases, final choices of music need to be made by the music minister, but other members of the team can make suggestions and offer ideas. The presider or homilist can use the sharing from this meeting to develop the preaching.

9. SUMMARIZE BY ASKING SOME BASIC QUESTIONS

What are our hopes for this celebration?
What do we hope this celebration will proclaim: About God? About faith? About the church?

10. END WITH PRAYER

Feel free to adapt this process to meet your needs. However, do not dismiss the need for some sort of process centered in prayer and Scripture, in which the overall liturgical and pastoral considerations are at the center of reflection and specific choices. There are many music ministers who work in isolation, unfortunately, without such collaboration with the priest or other members of the parish leadership as described above. Even alone, however, the music minister can find this process helpful in choosing repertoire and in implementation of that music in the ritual structure.

CHAPTER TEN

Issues and Challenges—Present and Future

PRESENT ISSUES

OFTEN, WHEN WE STRATEGIZE AND SEARCH for creative ways to encourage and empower assembly participation and ownership in the liturgical event, we forget to look first at some of our present practices and realities. It has been my experience that it is not so much that we need new, fancy and creative innovations, but that we need to take a good look at how we lead music and reflect upon some of the limitations and realities of our situations. Often, the solutions are not in discovering new tricks, but in taking an honest look at what we are already doing. However well-intentioned, many present approaches are at the root of the problem. I would like to address a few issues that I feel are serious detriments to life-giving liturgy and that should be of particular concern to parish music ministers.

A POVERTY OF HOSPITALITY

The unfortunate reality is that we actually do things in our liturgical celebrations and in our preparation that work against us. One of the primary expressions of this is the lack of hospitality in our parish churches. An important grounding in liturgy is that of hospitality. Most of us grew up being told that we were to be quiet and silent when we entered the worship space, to be "reverent" because we were in "God's house." How many times have you gone to someone's home for a party or celebration, and after the host or hostess opened the door, you were told to be quiet and silent because you were in their house? Most of us, when we host a celebration, welcome our guests with an embrace or greeting, offer to take their coats, offer them a drink, or invite them to help themselves and make themselves feel at home. This feeling of hospitality is lacking on a typical Sunday morning in most parishes, and is at the heart of the lack of attentiveness and participation. This lack of generous hospitality only tends to isolate people as individuals. We have generations of children (and more being trained in the same way at present) who have been taught to believe that church is a place to be quiet, that they better behave, shut up, not talk or share with those around and look straight ahead. At the same time, we have often shamed and scolded them when they do not sing or participate. Would it occur to us that perhaps we are sending a mixed and contradictory message?

I am not promoting a free-for-all before Mass begins, but I am asking all of us in liturgical ministry to help generate an atmosphere in which people can be free to greet one another. We need to help shape individual members of the assembly into becoming a cohesive family, a part of the Body of Christ. It has been my experience that parishes who take this issue seriously will in a few years have communities praying and celebrating passionately. At music ministry workshops and conferences that I have presented all across the country and other places, the most often asked question is: "How do we get the people to sing?" I believe this is the wrong question. The important issue is: "What do the people have to *sing about*?" When an assembly experiences themselves corporately as the community of believers rather than isolated individuals, when they feel bonded together on the journey of faith, then there is something to sing about. And as a result, they sing!

True hospitality is more than saying "Good morning. Welcome. It's great to see you here this morning"—although we have a long way to go to get many of our parishes to this point. Rather, true hospitality is as the late writer and teacher, Father Gene Walsh, S.S., used to love to say, "paying attention to one another." In other words, hospitality should say: "When you are not here, we are less the Body of Christ. When you are here, we are better as a result, and more completely the Body." With this, we truly reverence the presence of Christ—present, alive and breathing in the faces and presence of those who gather to worship with us. In other words, our call as baptized people is to be people who have the time, who take the time, who take the trouble to be present to one another.

MISSALETTES

I sometimes get raised eyebrows when I talk about this. But consider this for a moment. The priest prays from a wonderfully bound red book with gold leaf pages, and many lovely colored ribbons coming forth from the pages. The lector (reader) proclaims the Word of God from another beautifully bound book, rich with dignity. And what do the people get in many parishes? Cheap newspaper! And not only that, but a booklet that basically treats the worshipper like a child. The missalette has every single breath, word, gesture and text—far more than is needed. Beyond that, it stifles any kind of liturgical creativity, and basically is a short cut for those who do not want to take the hard work, time and energy necessary to prepare a quality celebration. Someone at some publishing house, who does not know you or your community, has planned the liturgy for you. Much of the music in some of these publications is extremely poor and badly crafted, and to top it all off, it is disposable (just like many in our assembly feel themselves to be), and we throw it away!

It is important to realize and accept the subliminal messages that can be sent to people. The questions here are: What does this kind of worship aid say about the assembly and their primacy as worshippers? What does this say about the dignity of the baptized? What does this say about liturgy being organic, creative and centered in the assembly? What does this say about the quality of the ministers? In the case of lectors, they do not have to worry about proclaiming the Word passionately and carefully because the people follow along rather than listening and taking the Word to heart. The presider (priest) does not have to engage people in a dialogue of praise because the entire dialogue, both the proclamation and the response, may be followed in print.

The musicians do not have to do research to develop the ritual repertoire for their community because it is already done for them.

Many excuses support the presence of the missalette. The first arguments often are "We do not have good lectors in our parish!" or "We have a rotten sound system!" These excuses are sad and really proclaim that we do not care about the quality of good reading. The answer is to train and form lectors well to become quality proclaimers of the Word. Good sound systems are fundamental for any worship space. Missalettes are not the answer. Their presence states support for poor ministry.

Another issue that comes up is the concern and consideration for people in the assembly who are hearing impaired. This is an important pastoral issue, but, again, the answer is not to continue to provide a missalette. The pastoral agenda for the parish in this case is to seek out the individuals who have the need and to provide them with materials that help them to be included in the worship experience. Many parishes have discovered that the answer here is to provide them with a Sunday missal of some kind, as a gift from the parish. Others say that the missalette can be a source for children to study and discuss with their parents the readings and other texts of the service. While the intention here is honorable, the point of Sunday worship is not to be a classroom, and the best way for children to learn the liturgy is to come to Mass every Sunday with their parents. Although discussion and further reflection is wonderful, that should be saved for another time. The final reason often stated for using the missalette for the assembly is that it is less expensive than other resources. In the long term, this is not true. A parish investing in a good strong hymnal or service book that contains only what is necessary for the worshipper, including an Order of Mass, is actually saving money over the long haul. This has been proven time and again.

The most significant danger of all presented by the missalette in the pew is that the missalette enables the assembly (and almost encourages them) to remain passive, to not be pulled outside themselves. The need for the assembly to have in their hands a detailed program destroys ritual and is in complete opposition to the essence of ritual. In my opinion, the presence of the missalette prevents many parish assemblies from being self-actualized and passionate "pray-ers" of the liturgy.

POOR ACOUSTICS

A fundamental principle in regard to participation is that if the assembly cannot hear each other, the environment is not conducive to strong participation. The common practice of carpeting worship spaces is an extreme abuse to an assembly struggling to find its voice in a participatory liturgy. When a room is carpeted, the reverberation of the space is diminished, if not completely obliterated. Lively participation flourishes in a space with good, strong reverberation. In this scenario, members of the assembly can hear their fellow worshippers and, thus, feel more comfortable with the sound of their own voice. Without reverberation, when one can hear only oneself, the result is a feeling of self-consciousness and a fear of "sticking out." Why is it that people love singing in the shower so much? It is because the acoustics enliven and enhance the voice and elevate it to some grandness and beauty. A parish should think long and hard before considering carpeting. While perhaps efficient for maintenance purposes, a carpeted floor has dire consequences for a parish that values participation (which should be *the* ultimate value). The contribution of good acoustics should rank higher in consideration than custodial and maintenance issues.

As stated before, a good sound system is critical for worship spaces, and such systems are largely misunderstood in their function. The issue is not volume but vocal enhancement that is hospitable for leaders and for assembly participation. The system should be evaluated for both spoken and sung words, and acoustical consultants and sound professionals need to be consulted.

PLACEMENT AND VESTURE OF MUSIC MINISTERS

Fundamentals of good leadership in any liturgical ministry include *visual* leadership. For music ministers, this is important and challenging, considering the architecture of many of our parish worship spaces. Parishes that still have a choir loft with the organ in the back of the worship space and sanctuaries with little or no space for music ministers have some unique challenges. But it must be stated clearly that the best music leadership will exist when the music is *seen* as well as heard.

Many of us remember the days when the priest had his back to us while praying in the sanctuary, the resulting experience being that the prayer appeared to be between himself and God, and we as the assembly were a passive audience who followed along in the missal. Imagine our present liturgy, with the priest with his back to us, as it was then, saying "The Lord be with you." If this were the case, there would be no sense of relationship, no dialogue, no feeling that this activity is something we do together.

The same is true with all of the ministries, and especially music ministry. Strong cantor leadership should be visible in front where the priest presides over the Eucharistic Prayer and other moments of the liturgy. The cantor, in a sense, presides over and leads the musical prayer of the assembly. The visual nature of musical leadership provides a sense of hospitality for the assembly, communicating an attitude that they are the primary ministers of music. The parish that has the challenge of an organ in the choir loft certainly has to work hard to achieve this availability of the cantor to the assembly. However, the effort of providing, at least, a single cantor in view of the assembly will be well worth the effort.

While there is no documentation or direction regarding the issue of robes or albs for the choir or cantors, I believe that wearing special attire does set these ministers apart from the assembly. I believe that robes can communicate an attitude (while not intended) of elitism and separateness. It is my strong feeling that the ministries should reflect and look like the assembly from which they arise. Often choir directors or choir members will say that they like the robes because then everyone will look the same. Why is this a goal? Why should we all look alike? We are *not* all alike! The people of our parishes are not alike in their appearance, in their tastes, political alliances and other aspects of their personality. This is the wonder of being church. Our diversity and pluralism is what makes up the Body of Christ. The choir and the cantor already are set apart by the very fact that they have a special elevated space from which they execute their ministry. It would seem that we should eliminate barriers and not encourage and create additional ones.

Theologically, the white alb is the symbol and garment of our baptism. If choir members, cantors, eucharistic ministers and others wear such garments, then the assembly should be invited to wear them as well, since baptism is our primary identity.

INFIGHTING BETWEEN DIFFERENT CAMPS

One of the greatest sources of sadness for our church is the "worship" or "style" wars that continue to plague our parish communities. The preoccupation and downright hurtful behaviors that exist still among ensembles, choirs and the people who are a part of these groups is shameful and should be seen as an embarrassment to the church at large. For some reason, different musical styles and genres present fear among musicians, and personal taste becomes a weapon for judgment, ridicule and division in our communities of faith.

In my travels and pastoral experience, the situation of non-civility between the so-called "traditional" and "contemporary" music ministers has gotten worse in recent years. Pastors and parish music directors should proclaim a zero tolerance policy toward what I deliberately name as evil behavior. When efforts toward reconciliation and amends are not taken seriously, when sabotage and intentional gossiping and hurtful actions continue after such efforts are in place, the perpetrators of these activities should no longer be allowed to stand and minister amid the parish community.

SPECIFIC LITURGICAL MOMENTS AND CHOICES

There is a big difference between intentions and perceptions. In other words, what a person may intend to communicate is not always what another may receive. This is important when we reflect upon and evaluate what we do in the liturgy. When we look at specific liturgical moments throughout the liturgy, we need first to study and discuss what the actual intention of the ritual moment is, and then ask ourselves whether or not that intention is being carried out by the choices we make. When this reflection is absent we can communicate an attitude or message that is contradictory to our intent. The liturgy is not a perfect event, and the consequences of not examining our effects can be that the assembly begins to believe something about themselves, about the liturgy, that is actually the opposite of what the liturgy proclaims. These consequences that may seem to be non-musical issues actually affect our sung prayer in many ways.

There are many examples that could be cited. The point of reflecting upon what we intend to communicate and what we actually communicate is always to be aware of the liturgy's immense power. The liturgy communicates much to the assembly about their status in the liturgical enterprise. When that status is damaged, the real work and challenge for musicians and liturgists is immense, and is often the root cause of liturgy's not being a life-giving and nurturing experience. We musicians have a unique gift to help the assembly give voice to their faith, and to ignore these issues will have grave consequences in the quality of our ministry. The call to empower the assembly to see and experience themselves as church, as the living embodiment of the presence of Christ in service to the world and to the building of God's reign, is part and parcel of our missionary role.

CHALLENGES FOR THE FUTURE

There are at present many movements, developments and trends in the areas of music, liturgy and parish life in general that ministers of music need to reflect on as we embark on the future. We live in a culture of individualism, entertainment, capitalism and self-absorption which exists in opposition to what liturgy and our entire life of faith proclaim. Our lack of lament in worship and the widening divide between authentic worship and the mandate of Catholic social teaching is severely lacking. The rise of technology has tremendous consequences for ritual as machines, computers and sequencers are more frequently replacing human beings as music makers. We live in a world where therapy is often the goal of liturgical worship, rather than true and honest spiritual growth. The gift of ecumenism that exploded at the Second Vatican Council seems to be diminishing and the divide between Christians deepens an angry and conservative backlash is being preached by many Catholic leaders who feel threatened by the openness of renewal, especially in the liturgy. The attack upon inclusive language, the critique of multicultural diversity and lay leadership is driving many people—women, the elderly, the physically and mentally challenged, and people of different cultures—away from our church as they feel they are not welcomed and honored for who they are and what they experience. The youth of our church continue to feel held at the margins of liturgical and parish life in general, resorting to programs and movements that liturgically and catechetically separate them and create a divided community of faith. The ongoing denial of the church to face the real crisis of priestless parishes is serious. The result is an ongoing absence of Sunday Eucharist for many communities, or the development of mega-parishes where true community is almost impossible to develop and nurture. These and many other issues are now and will continue to provide real challenges for those involved in liturgy and music.

If we dwell on these problems too intensely, we can become discouraged and hopeless. But to retreat and not to face them is also to be in denial and to become apathetic and to reject our prophetic role. Discipleship means to face the Paschal Mystery, not only in our personal spiritual path, but to struggle and remain faithful to it in the midst of pain and growth in the church. A church that is not in crisis will never grow, and we need to see and embrace these challenges and concerns not as roadblocks and ending points in the road, but rather as a new highway to build for the sake of the reign of God.

POSTLUDE

IN THE PRELUDE to this book and throughout the subsequent chapters, I have addressed passionately the need for ministers of music to embrace a metaphor of mission in our approach as ministers of sung prayer. It is my fervent hope that this resource in some way has stirred up the need to reexamine our efforts and our skills, and resulted in a recommitment to a more authentic vision of service as liturgical musicians.

But now, I want to speak about joy. I believe that we need to reinstill a true sense of joy in our ministry of music, within ourselves and in the people we serve. Somehow, and sometimes, we have lost the sense of true joy, so that we see our ministry and service as drudgery, a job or something that we are destined to endure rather than celebrate with every depth of our being. Part of ministerial renewal is to continually reexamine this basic tenet of what baptism proclaims for us. So, let us go forth with a fresh look at the story of God's joy:

In the beginning,
God gave us all something to sing about.
At the dawn of creation,
music filled the air!
All creatures,
all the animals who crawl,
creep, swim and slide,
were born with sounds and noises,
proclaiming their existence!
All of the galaxies,
the heavens and the earth,
echoed their joy through their song!

Then the breath of life came
into woman and man—
what a song!
A song of mind, heart,
body and soul;
of relationship,
the laments of stumbling,
longing and repentance;
and the true rejoicing
of reconciliation,

connection and new birth.
God gave them reason to sing,
for paradise was all around them,
inescapable,
unconditionally offering
blessing upon blessing
upon blessing.
The blessing at times turned
to mourning,
but joy kept returning,
for this gift was non-returnable,
and the song kept coming.

Then God led people to sing
and dream about a promised land;
a land not only flowing
with milk and honey,
but a place, space
and way of life
that was filled with song.
God gave them songs
to lift them from their fear,
their sorrow,
their hopelessness
and the imprisonment of themselves.
The songs were shared with their children,
and songs, psalms, canticles were
the beginnings of a new story,
a new vision,
a new promise.

In Jesus,
God gave us a new song;
Mary offered the overture,
with joy unsurpassed,
presenting us with the steps,
the notes and the words
to embrace the wonder of
liberation, justice
and freedom from terror.
The angels sang
like never before: "Glory!"

The Ministry and Mission of Sung Prayer

Jesus sang,
boy, did he sing!
He sang joy,
he sang challenge,
he sang hope,
he sang life!
He sang with friends
and invited the outcast
to join the choir;
gave them a voice
that they never knew they had.
There was never music like this,
because this music
told the story that our
suffering, oppression,
anxiety and human sinfulness
was not the true song.
Jesus led us in the song
to embrace our suffering
as a prelude to life;
that the strains of death
lead us to the sustained
and lasting symphony of heaven!

Jesus was the ultimate
minister of music—
he was from their community;
lived, laughed, ached,
struggled, endured all and even
took on their lives as his own.
He sang on their behalf,
he composed, created,
prepared and lived the music.
The music was honest,
authentic,
and one that all people
were invited to own,
sing and live by.

He had a great choir—
albeit a "human" and
imperfect ensemble;
calling them disciples,
friends.

They rehearsed,
rehearsed and practiced
(sometimes more fervently
than other times)
to keep the song
young, vibrant and true.
The choir kept growing,
and God is still inviting
people to join.
God wants us to remember
the song of Jesus;
wanting us to remember
the great song of love:
that no matter how we have failed,
no matter how often we stumble,
no matter how much
we become discouraged,
the song is still there to sing,
because it is the truth.

We need singers and players
to keep the joy in the faces
of our people.
We need voices and instruments
to give us rhythms and notes
to dance the new steps
that God keeps creating
and designing for us.
We need minstrels and songsters
to keep us singing,
to keep us hopeful,
to keep us alive.

You and I,
yes, you and I
are the inheritors of this music,
of the canticle of freedom and peace
that can only come through this song.
Most songs come and go,
lose their popularity,
are sung for a while.
But this song is life everlasting.
This song is the pathway
for all that we hope is possible.

This song is the rope
that we hang on to as we weep
and long for something better.

We will most assuredly
get discouraged
when others refuse to sing along.
We will obviously
become frustrated when
no one appreciates our
practicing,
our planning,
our ideas,
our creativity.
But, if we are open,
if we are attentive,
we will see muted voices
become released;
with songs and words
more in tune,
more in sync,
more beautiful.

Let us remain joyful,
let us take the risk again
to offer our enthusiasm,
our joy, our energy,
and truly sing to the Lord
a new song!
Let us "make things new" again,
and compose, sing,
share, dance
and breathe life into new songs,
new prayers,
new metaphors,
and help shape and create
a renewed litany of rejoicing.

If we have lost the joy,
we need to pray to God
to crack us open,
to find an open door
where our heart can again
be melted into this loving embrace.

For we need remember,
music does not belong to us—
it was, is, and will always be
God's idea,
God's plan,
God's composition;
and we are God's work of art!
With our music,
our hands
and our voices,
let us truly go forward
rejoicing to the house of the Lord!

INDEX